⊚)SCORPIO(⊚
24 OCTOBER – 22 NOVEMBER

First published in Great Britain 2011
by Mills & Boon, an imprint of Harlequin (UK) Limited,
Eton House, 18-24 Paradise Road, Richmond, Surrey TW9 1SR

Copyright © Dadhichi Toth 2011

ISBN: 978 0 263 89658 9

Design by Jo Yuen Graphic Design
Typeset by KDW DESIGNS

Harlequin (UK) policy is to use papers that are natural, renewable and recyclable products and made from wood grown in sustainable forests. The logging and manufacturing processes conform to the legal environmental regulations of the country of origin.

Printed and bound in Spain
by Blackprint CPI, Barcelona

Dedicated to

The Light of Intuition

Sri V. Krishnaswamy—mentor and friend

With thanks to

Joram and Isaac

Special thanks to

Nyle Cruz for

initial creative layouts and ongoing support

ABOUT DADHICHI

Dadhichi is one of Australia's foremost astrologers and is frequently seen on television and in other media. He has the unique ability to draw from complex astrological theory to provide clear, easily understandable advice and insights for people who want to know what their futures may hold.

In the 26 years that Dadhichi has been practising astrology, face reading and other esoteric studies, he has conducted over 10,000 consultations. His clients include celebrities, political and diplomatic figures, and media and corporate identities from all over the world.

Dadhichi's unique blend of astrology and face reading helps people fulfil their true potential. His extensive experience practising Western astrology is complemented by his research into the theory and practice of Eastern forms of astrology.

Dadhichi has been a guest on many Australian television shows, and several of his political and worldwide forecasts have proved uncannily accurate. He appears regularly on Australian television networks and is a columnist for online and offline Australian publications.

His websites—www.dadhichi.com and www.facereader. com—attract hundreds of thousands of visitors each month, and offer a wide variety of features, helpful information and services.

MESSAGE FROM
◎ DADHICHI ◎

Hello once again and welcome to your 2012 horoscope book!

Can you believe it's already 2012? Time flies by so quickly and now here we are in this fateful year, a time for which several religions of the world—including the Mayans from 3100BC—have predicted some extraordinary events that are supposedly going to affect us all!

Some people are worried there will be a physical cataclysm that will kill millions and millions. Some are of the opinion it is the end of the economic and social models we have lived by for thousands of years. Others seem to believe the Planet Nibiru will whiz by planet Earth and beam up the 144,000 Chosen Ones.

Whatever the opinion, it is an undeniable fact that we are experiencing some remarkable worldwide changes due to global warming (even though that remains a point of contention) and other societal shifts. Scientific knowledge continues to outrun our ability to keep up with it, and time appears to be moving faster and faster.

But my own research has categorically led me to repeat: 'Relax, everyone; it is *not* the end of the world!' There will most certainly be a backlash at some point by Mother Earth at the gross unconsciousness of many of us. There will be ravaging storms, earthquakes and other meteorological phenomena that will shake the Earth, hopefully waking up those of us still in a deep sleep, dreaming, or possibly even sleepwalking. It is time to open our eyes and take responsibility.

If there are any significant global changes I foresee, they are the emergence of wider self-government and the greater Aquarian qualities of the coming New Age. This period is the cusp or changeover between the Age of Pisces, the Fish, and the Age of Aquarius, the Dawn of Higher Mankind.

Astrology, and these small books I write about it, are for the sole purpose of shedding light on our higher selves, alerting us to the need to evolve, step up to the plate, and assume responsibility for our thoughts, words and deeds, individually and collectively. The processes of karma are ripe now as we see the Earth's changes shouting to us about our past mistakes as a civilisation.

I hope you gain some deeper insight into yourself through these writings. For the 2012 series I have extended the topics and focused more on relationships. It is only through having a clear perception of our responsibility towards others that we can live the principles of astrology and karma to reach our own self-actualisation, both as individuals and as a race.

I hope you see the light of truth within yourself and that these words will act as a pointer in your ongoing search.

All the best for 2012.

Your Astrologer,

www.dadhichi.com
dadhichitoth@gmail.com
Tel: +61 (0) 413 124 809

◎ CONTENTS ◎

◎ CONTENTS ◎

⊚ CONTENTS ⊚
CONTINUED

SCORPIO
PROFILE

AH, BUT A MAN'S REACH SHOULD
EXCEED HIS GRASP, OR WHAT'S A
HEAVEN FOR?

Robert Browning

⚹ SCORPIO SNAPSHOT ⚹

Key Life Phrase		I Will
Zodiac Totem		The Scorpion, the Grey Lizard and the Phoenix
Zodiac Symbol	♏	
Zodiac Facts		Eighth sign of the zodiac; fixed, fruitful, feminine and moist
Zodiac Element		Water
Key Characteristics		Secretive, passionate, resolute, insensitive, steadfast, painstaking and stubborn
Compatible Star Signs		Taurus, Cancer, Virgo, Scorpio, Sagittarius, Capricorn and Pisces
Mismatched Signs		Aries, Gemini, Leo, Libra and Aquarius
Ruling Planets		Mars and Pluto

Love Planets		Venus, Jupiter and Neptune
Finance Planet		Jupiter
Speculation Planets		Jupiter and Neptune
Career Planet		Sun
Spiritual and Karmic Planets		Moon, Jupiter and Neptune
Friendship Planet		Mercury
Destiny Planets		Jupiter and Neptune
Famous Scorpios		Leonardo DiCaprio, Ethan Hawke, Sean 'Diddy' Combs, Owen Wilson, Ryan Gosling, Gavin Rossdale, Bill Gates, Joaquin Phoenix, Gerard Butler, Ryan Reynolds, Matthew McConaughey, David Schwimmer, Jodie Foster, Anne Hathaway, Winona Ryder, Demi Moore, Jenny McCarthy, Meg Ryan, Calista Flockhart, Vivien Leigh, Julia Roberts, Kelly Osbourne, Gabrielle Union and Grace Kelly

Lucky Numbers and Significant Years	2, 3, 9, 11, 12, 18, 20, 21, 27, 29, 30, 36, 38, 45, 47, 48, 54, 56, 57, 74, 75, 81, 83 and 84
Lucky Gems	Red coral, garnet, red spinel, ruby and yellow sapphire
Lucky Fragrances	Cinnamon, pine, cypress, lime and black pepper
Affirmation/ Mantra	I don't need to control *everything*. I am free and peaceful
Lucky Days	Monday, Tuesday, Thursday and Sunday

SCORPIO
⊚ OVERVIEW ⊚

Scorpios usually don't require too much of an introduction—most people already know of the intensity of this star sign. But it is worth mentioning some of the extraordinary personality traits you possess, Scorpio, especially for those who are not aware of the esoteric significance of your birth sign.

First and foremost, the sign of Scorpio, being the eighth sign of the zodiac, rules such things as life, death and, most importantly, regeneration and self-transformation.

Ordinarily, Scorpio is depicted as the Scorpion, which is its totem. However, other astrological writers assign two other totems as well—the Grey Lizard and the Phoenix—to symbolise the gamut of different people who fall under your Sun sign.

The Phoenix represents your capacity to metamorphose, to rise above the limitations of your star sign; but this, of course, involves death before rebirth. So I'm not literally speaking of physical death here, but one where you totally transform your personality from that of an ordinary person to someone who is self-actualised. This is the true significance of Scorpio, not only as your birth sign, but also as a principle relating to the evolution of humanity.

Scorpios are sometimes considered secretive, and yes, they are, to some extent. But the secrets we're alluding to are those of nature, life and spirituality.

Because your birth was under the sign of secret holding, you are fascinated by anything relating to psychology, religion, meditation and other forms of evolutionary self-development.

Through these methods, you are able to develop your capacity to go beyond yourself, and if you are this type of Scorpio, then we can assume that the Phoenix is fully reflected in this stage of your evolution.

However, for those of you still in the clutches of the Scorpion, you have a way to go yet, and will be the type of Scorpio who uses his or her energy in ways that are not so becoming of their better attributes.

Scorpio's Dark Side

Jealousy, possessiveness and vengeance are some of the negative traits associated with this side of your Sun sign.

But whether you are at the stage of the Scorpion or the Phoenix, you have an extraordinarily powerful tongue, and your speech can be used to uplift or destroy. You can be highly critical of others, particularly of those you dislike.

The third totem, which is not so well known, is that of the Grey Lizard. This Scorpionic type tends to withdraw into itself, and may have an addictive personality. Because Scorpio is, for the most part, intense, sometimes impulsive, obsessive traits relating to drinking, smoking and drug abuse are manifested as excuses to get through life.

SEXUAL SCORPIO!

Irrespective of which of the three Scorpio totems relate to you, sex will always be an important part of your life, and you tend to express yourself most ably through this activity.

Sexuality is also another key word for the sign of Scorpio, and the eighth zone of the horoscope represents this force of your nature most adequately.

You are deliberate, wilful, energetic and powerful in every sense of these words. Your willpower is a force to be reckoned with, and when you decide upon a course of action, your courage will help you break through any of the obstacles that life presents. There's no greater satisfaction for a Scorpio than achieving success in their chosen field or endeavour. Nothing can stop you from achieving your objectives.

Your eyes are part of your magnetic and sexual appeal, and people find you enigmatic. Being difficult to understand, you use this to your advantage, and can control and dominate others. Be careful to use these extraordinary powers in positive ways, however, rather than abusing them.

⊚ SCORPIO CUSPS ⊚

ARE YOU A CUSP BABY?

Being born on the changeover of two star signs means you have the qualities of both. Sometimes you don't know whether you're Arthur or Martha, as they say! Some of my clients can't quite figure out if they are indeed their own star sign, or the one before, or after. This is to be expected because being born on the borderline means you take on aspects of both. The following outlines give an overview of the subtle effects of these cusp dates and how they affect your personality quite significantly.

Scorpio-Libra Cusp

If you were born in the period between October the 24th and November the 1st, then you fall in the area of the zodiac jointly ruled by Libra and Scorpio. Together these star signs are ruled by Venus, Mars and Pluto.

The intensity of Scorpio is somewhat balanced by the sign of Libra, and makes you even more attractive and pleasing to others, especially potential lovers. You have great people skills and a need to help others through your intuitive understanding.

You love excitement, and the pleasure-seeking aspect of your nature combined with the social skills of Libra makes you a social butterfly who can attract loads of friends in both social and professional arenas.

BEST AND WORST!

The best and worst traits of both signs will be exhibited
by you. You have a great deal of determination,
a powerful self-control, and excellent psychic and
intuitive abilities.

The social and superficial attributes of Libra are counteracted by the serious and philosophical characteristics of Scorpio.

You have an extraordinary intelligence and insight into human nature. However, your sharp tongue and straightforward opinions sometimes make you feared by others—you don't mince words when you offer your critique on personal, social or political issues.

Some people feel you have an extraordinarily big ego. You probably happily agree with them, so this doesn't worry you in the least. You have a charismatic personality and expect to make some enemies along the way. You aren't bothered about this shortcoming, because the huge number of people you have as allies and friends outdoes the number of antagonists in the background.

You're an expert in communication and have wonderful reasoning powers. You're a strong lover of family and support the people you love, sacrificing anything and everything to maintain their security.

Scorpio-Sagittarius Cusp

If you happen to be born between the 15th and the 21st of November, you will show traits of both Scorpio and Sagittarius. Some astrologists may disagree with these dates, but in actual fact, you'll find that you do, in practice, possess characteristic traits of both signs to a greater or lesser degree.

Your intense Scorpio traits are finely balanced by the easygoing, magnanimous spirit of Sagittarius. Those of you born during this period are ruled by Mars, Pluto and Jupiter, the latter being the ruler of Sagittarius. You have an optimistic nature, but can be rather aggressive in achieving your goals. You are constantly on the go, working with zeal to achieve your dreams.

Your magnetic personality is accentuated even further by the popular and outgoing Jupiter. You have a brilliant sense of timing, and will meet the right people at the right time to help you get to where you're going.

You are an emotionally deep person and, coupled with the Sagittarian honesty and generosity, are the type of person to whom people open their hearts and trust easily. You will always be there to help others and are even considered somewhat of a teacher. You are constantly driving and advising others—friends and strangers alike—in the way they should proceed when floundering in their life problems.

You are an extraordinarily independent person, and hate to be contained by anyone. You are quite wild and fun loving, but this should taper off as you get a little older.

You are excessive in your life and must be careful not to overdo things. You work, live and play hard. You need to pay more attention to your physical needs, because at times you overdo it, and your health is prone to suffer.

SCORPIO
✕ CELEBRITIES ✕

FAMOUS MALE:
LEONARDO DICAPRIO

Leonardo DiCaprio is a blockbuster name in Hollywood, and he can now earn up to $20 million per movie. He achieved great heights with his first success, *Titanic,* which led to bigger and better roles, bringing with them accolades and respect from fans and peers alike.

Leonardo was born on the 11th of November, 1974, in Hollywood, California. He is a true Scorpio, and exhibits his Scorpio traits through his intense involvement in acting.

He has often spoken of his love of acting, which allows him the opportunity to transcend his day-to-day personality and lose himself in a new character. This aspect of transforming one's nature is very Scorpionic, indeed.

Some of the other films that Leonardo has appeared in include *The Beach* and *Romeo +*

Juliet, *Critters 3*, which was a low-budget horror movie, and the sitcom *Growing Pains*.

I personally love Leonardo DiCaprio's quotes, which seem to reveal the very powerful Scorpio personality that he possesses. Here are a few of them:

'You can either be a vain movie star, or you can try to shed some light on different aspects of the human condition.'

'I'm not really the quiet type, although some people think I am. But I am the rebel type in the sense that I don't think I'm like everyone else. I try to be an individual.'

'I like to help the whales, the otters and the dolphins. When I'm acting and I take a break, the first thing on my list is spending time by the sea.'

I like the last quote, especially because it refers to the ocean, the water and nature. Many Scorpio-born individuals do indeed love to spend time near the water, because Scorpio is, of course, a water sign.

LEONARDO'S COMPLEX ROLES

It's interesting to note that Leonardo's roles are often complex self-tortured or conflicted personality types, which, in part, seems to reflect his Scorpio birth sign.

FAMOUS FEMALE:
DEMI MOORE

Like Leonardo DiCaprio, Demi Moore was also born on the 11th of November, but in Roswell, New Mexico, in 1962. Her trademark husky voice symbolises the sensual and magnetic energy of the Scorpio female. This sexy quality has always been a part of her film and acting career, and has made her almost a goddess to her fans worldwide. Demi, like many Scorpio females, is not afraid to use her sexuality to turn others on. She revels in this gift, and has used it successfully in her professional life.

Her desire to find happiness in love is an important feature of her life, which can be seen in the fact that she's been married three times—first to Freddy Moore in 1980, then to Bruce Willis in 1987 (with whom she had three children), and, more recently, in 2005 to the younger Ashton Kutcher. This reflects the high degree of energy and sexuality found in Scorpio and, in particular, in the females of this star sign.

DEMI'S BOLDNESS

Like many Scorpios, Demi uses shock tactics to deliver her ideologies and opinions. This she did when she posed nude—when seven months' pregnant—in 1991, for the cover of Vanity Fair. This was quite an eye-opener for fans, and for people generally. She did the same thing in 1992, posing nude again, only this time painting her body in what looked like a man's suit.

To make a point, she actually stripped on *The Late Show with David Letterman* in 1993, after some of the gossip magazines accused her of being overweight. This proved her critics wrong!

One of my favourite quotes of Demi Moore's, that reflects her true Scorpionic nature is: 'Time is an amazing equalizer. I think if you stay true to yourself and keep moving forward, things come around.'

Once again, this indicates the determined nature of the Scorpio individual, and Demi Moore truly does represent this element of Scorpio to the max.

SCORPIO

AT LARGE

YOU MUST LOOK INTO OTHER
PEOPLE AS WELL AS AT THEM.

Lord Chesterfield

⊚ SCORPIO MAN ⊚

♂

SCORPIO MAN: SNAPSHOT

Powerful

Magnetic

Sexual

Manipulative

Enigmatic

The Scorpio male is an enigma to most people, but none greater than himself. The energy of Scorpio is difficult to deal with, and those born under it, including you, if you're reading this, will understand exactly what I'm talking about.

Scorpio men are born with a powerful, intuitive nature, and live largely by their gut feelings. If you meet a Scorpio male and, for some reason, he doesn't like you, even if you haven't done anything wrong, you simply have to accept the fact he will not be easy to win over, if at all. His sensitivity dominates his mental judgements, and therefore he is not easy to get close to.

A Scorpio man is often found to be self-absorbed, wrapped up in his own sense of self. Being a Scorpio male, you demand a lot, both of yourself and others, and you hate it when you fall short of the mark. You're extremely self-critical because you set yourself such high standards.

Other people find you hard to understand, yet this air of mystery is what often attracts them. Even if they never understand you, the desire to get close to you keeps them coming back for more and more.

You can be an extremely successful person. But remember, it can and will get lonely at the top. You don't trust others that easily, and even though you may, in the early part of your life, draw people close to you and put much faith in them, you will become a little more cynical as you get older, realising that human nature is not all that you hoped it would be.

 Tenacious Scorpio

It's hard to describe the tenacity and forbearance of a Scorpio, but let me say this: a Scorpio male, once he sets his mind to a task, will never give up, even if it takes years. This also goes for his vengeful nature, if that is ever roused. A Scorpio man never forgets a kindness, nor a hurt. He will make good his promise to set aright any wrongdoing to him or the ones he loves.

The Scorpio male is a sexual creature and needs love, passion and attention as his primary fuel in life. If you are a woman reading this, you must understand that his motivations are far more complex and demanding than the average male. To read more on this, look at the later section on Scorpio's romantic nature.

Although you are considered the strong, silent type, Scorpio, there are moments when people are totally astounded by the way you articulate your thoughts and beliefs. You're not a follower, you're a leader, and this is shown in the way you communicate your ideas.

You love to make an impact on others, and can tell a great story. You must, however, guard against letting your ego get the better of you, because you have a tendency to take control of social situations, and be a little insensitive to the need for others to have their say as well. Nevertheless, you're always popular, and people are fascinated by what you have to say and the way in which you say it.

Although you are loyal and protect your loved ones, you also wish to possess them. This can make life difficult—for you and for them—if they are not as intense as you. You tend to see a lack of intensity as weakness. But try to remember that not everyone has your level of energy, and that less energy doesn't necessarily equal less passion, love or commitment.

You have an interesting philosophical and sexual mix inside you, Scorpio. In this respect, you're sometimes torn between your desire to express your sexuality through your supreme seduction techniques, and your yearning to reach a higher plateau of spiritual awareness through meditation, self-awareness and even great athletic sacrifice.

This tension, believe it or not, actually works in your favour, with people attracted to the complexity of your mind.

You have the ability to charm anyone and everyone, and pride yourself on your self-control and ability to win over others.

You'd like to enjoy yourself without limitations, of course, but as mentioned in the introduction, you have a penchant for food, alcohol and sex. All these are fine, as long as you partake of them in moderation.

SCORPIO MEMORY
Scorpio men have wonderful minds, and they remember the smallest details for years and years. Self-respect and respect from others is highly valued— above all, they want to be admired.

You should never cross a Scorpio male because his temper can be explosive and unrelenting. When the Scorpion strikes, he strikes to kill. Non-Scorpios reading this should take note, because they can exhibit this personality trait in general discussion. They hate to be proved wrong, and can react quite strongly.

You're a man who doesn't really care what others think, Scorpio, but there are times when it would be more helpful to toe the line and act like others do, even if you think differently.

SCORPIO WOMAN

SCORPIO WOMAN: SNAPSHOT

Loyal

Practical

Sensual

Demanding

Original

Probably one of the most sexually alluring and attractive women of the zodiac is the Scorpio female. Being a Scorpio woman means that you often prefer to speak with your body language and, in particular, with your eyes, to express the complexity of your emotions and state of mind. That air of mystery you exude attracts others, but there are some who are also fearful of it, because they prefer to deal with a more straightforward personality. This doesn't bother you, and your motto is more than likely: 'Take me as I am, or take a hike.'

You're a confident woman, and this comes from years of life experience. You grow up quickly and are exposed to much that others have never dreamt of. This wealth of experience, coupled with your inbuilt gifts of intuition, logic and deduction, gives you the edge over others, and you use it to propel yourself forwards and put yourself in dominant positions.

Pride and individuality, along with your fiercely independent nature, make you a difficult individual to live with. To large extent, you are a law unto yourself, and, interestingly, you find the difficulty others have in dealing with you to be the perfect way to maintain control over them.

You always look great; you enjoy life and can casually disarm others. Although you hide your feelings, the way you present yourself seems innocent and harmless enough. Little do others know!

A Tempestuous Nature

In terms of dealing with others, Scorpio, you have a suspicious nature, and your temper, too, can flare up in an instant. Little things can cause you to brood and others may be totally oblivious to what they've done to trigger the black mood that often arises. Please try to take control of this, as it can slowly erode even the best relationships you have.

Being independent, you like to work hard for your money, and earn well you will. You like nothing more than lavishly spending the money you accumulate. Your reputation, the finer things in life, and a high level of self-esteem cause you to stand out among the crowd of mediocrity.

You achieve a lot in life and, at the same time, don't expect anyone to hand you anything on a silver plate.

You are the seducer of the zodiac, so there's never a time when you feel as if the world doesn't desire you. Your magnetism seems to attract people from all walks of life.

You can keep a secret, which is why friends often confide in you. Even if you don't have a lot to say, your presence makes them feel better. Your aura has a healing quality, and people like to draw on your energy.

Although you are possessive, you are also generous to a fault. There is an unexpected side to this: if someone doesn't demand too much of you, you'll give them the world. You like to help people, especially if they are in need, because helping seems the natural thing to do. You are a humanitarian at heart, but not in the conventional sense.

 Seductive, Loving Scorpio

Making others feel great—especially in the areas of sex and romance—is one of your greatest gifts. No one can beat you there! You're a born lover and you'll bring pleasure to many people in your life.

You're happy to work for what you earn and have. When others get to know you, you exhibit a hard, almost masculine quality, and men should indeed tread warily in your company. In fact, you may overcompensate to prove you're just as powerful as they are. You may just be, indeed, but try to balance these masculine qualities with the feminine traits of seductiveness, charm and magnetic appeal. This approach will work as well as, if not better than, the hardnosed one you often prefer.

And lastly, you're an intuitive person who can come up with solutions without any intellectual effort. This is second nature to you.

You have a wonderfully accurate psychic ability, and need not go to the extra trouble of researching facts and figures to get an understanding of someone or something. You usually know instantaneously whether your sixth sense is correct or not.

⊚ SCORPIO CHILD ⊚

Your Scorpio child has an immensely strong character, and you'll need to set some clear guidelines for him or her at the earliest possible age. Failing to do this will create many problems for you as your child grows.

Because Scorpio is ruled by Mars and Pluto, a young Scorpion is full of energy and drive, is intelligent, and is curious about anything and everything. They are particularly competitive and love any sport in which they can assert their superiority over others.

Your young Scorpio wants to prove their worth by being the best at what they attempt. They are persistent and determined to prove that, even against great odds, they can be supremely victorious. And they usually are.

Scorpio children have a strong body and the resilience to go with it. But they are also prone to injury because they have a daredevil nature. Dangerous sports, skylarking and other outdoor activities that put them in harm's way should be monitored or discouraged—lest they have any physical mishaps.

Scorpio children surround themselves with many other children, having a magnetic personality and the ability to charm others. Having said that, they are also likely to have many run-ins and altercations—their egos are quite strong and they like to be the leader, not the follower. This will cause them social problems, and you need to teach them the joy of serving as well as being in control.

They dream of doing something no one else has done before, like Superman or Superwoman. Why not buy them a chemistry or electronics set (or something equally challenging), and let them play out their fantasies of greatness through invention and discovery?

Young Scorpio girls love to cook and make up recipes with their parents. Scorpio boys are competitive and do well in sports, particularly where stamina is required. They usually come out on top in any sporting activity in which they're involved.

Scorpio kids make excellent friends because they are loyal and focused, but they do always need to be the centre of attention. If they aren't the kingpin in one group, they'll move on to another—in fact, to anyone who will crown them as leader.

They're quick and intuitive learners, and should be encouraged to do subjects in which they are naturally interested. If they are not supported this way, they can become lazy and develop the habit of taking the shortest route through everything in life.

Argumentative Scorpio

The Scorpio child's mind is highly developed, and they're able to communicate just as easily as some adults. In fact, you'll be stumped at times, when they give you good reasons for why they should have their own way.

You can expect your fair share of disagreements with them as well. If you're not well prepared, you'll be rather embarrassed, and may not be able to assert your parental authority over them. That would be a big mistake, so you must never let that happen. You need to be strong—fair but firm—and you need to encourage them in their interests without forcing them to do the things that you think are best suited to them.

You need, above all, to bear in mind that they have an attraction to the dark side of life. As they move into their teen years, please be aware that drugs, sexuality and various vices may hold some appeal for them. If you educate them earlier rather than later, you'll be better able to help them avoid the pitfalls associated with such negative forms of behaviour.

⊚ SCORPIO LOVER ⊚

Scorpios, both men and women, have mastered the art of seduction. Yes, Scorpio, you are the supreme lover of the zodiac, and I think it's safe for me to echo the thoughts of many practitioners before me (and laypeople alike) who will attest to this. You are indeed an amazing lover and an intense partner once you have given your heart to the person of your choice.

Love, for you, is not simply a day-by-day routine, which is unfortunately what happens in many relationships. For you, the essence of love is a creative impulse that you are impelled to share with that special person. You'd like them to travel this path of romance with you and share the heights of ecstasy: almost religious transformation through the process of sharing your love, your minds and your bodies with each other.

Many Scorpios love to test their ability with potential partners by seeing just how many people they can seduce. Sexuality, for you, is a means of testing your magnetism, your appeal. Even if you're in a relationship and are fully committed, you're often curious as to whether or not you've maintained your edge.

Scorpio is generally secretive, but in matters of love and romance, you are extremely demonstrative. You love to show your feelings once you have chosen a lover, and you need to have your affection reciprocated.

Being born under the most sexual sign, you are dynamic, emotional and complex in love, so anyone who gets involved with you must be prepared for a bit of a challenge. If they can tread the path with you, they will be transformed by the process. Love with a Scorpio is thrilling, and never dull.

Many people who don't know you well are afraid of your intensity, the way you dive into relationships. From your perspective, it's just that you know what you want from someone, so you don't waste any time. Everyone you connect with gets a sense of assurance and security from that confidence.

Although I speak as if the typical Scorpio has a licentious nature, I only say this because it is, indeed, part of the Scorpio nature. But let me add to this, by saying that the loyalty of the Scorpio is pretty hard to beat. Once Scorpio has deemed another person to be their mate, they will go to the ends of the Earth to prove their love and sincerity for them.

Scorpios give their all to the one they love. You would be extremely fortunate to be in a relationship with a Scorpio, if you can honour their rare commitment by responding in a like manner. But if you slack off, take your Scorpio's love and fidelity for granted, or dismiss or reject them, I'll say to you right now that it will be a grave mistake.

Not only does a Scorpio withdraw their love just as quickly as they've given it, irrespective of how much they have invested in a relationship, but they will also make you suffer for that withdrawal of attention and affection. Yes, you will, unfortunately, have to deal with the darker forces of Scorpio in love.

THE DARKER SCORPIO

*As we move to the deeper, more complex aspects of
Scorpio's love nature, we find negative traits such as
envy, possessiveness, manipulation and control in the
mix. Now, not all Scorpios exhibit these traits, but to a
greater or lesser extent, you will find them to be part
and parcel of their personalities.*

How you deal with your jealousy is an issue for both you, Scorpio, and for your partner. It will stem from your insecurities and vulnerabilities, perhaps from childhood. You must do your best not to have this visit upon your relationship because it could result in an incredible pulling back by the one you love most.

In this way, your relationship must be based on trust, not manipulation and control, which will only serve to— inhibit and eventually destroy—the very thing you are trying to achieve.

 Room to Breathe

Scorpios must give their partners sufficient room to breathe, and offer them the independence that they also demand from them.

Your partner must be someone who's prepared to grow in love with you. In this sense, you expect them to act their best, look their best and satisfy each and every one of your needs. If your partner is up to the task, they won't be disappointed in the way you return that love. The Scorpio love, once it's for real, is supreme.

You can be moody and brooding and hard for your partner to figure out. You'll often seem withdrawn, and won't share your thoughts. And you sometimes shut down, especially when you're stressed or emotionally deprived. This can be very hard for the people around you.

Unless you give your lover a hint about what is bothering you, you could end up pushing them further and further away. Reach out and explain your feelings as much as you can.

The other water signs, Pisces and Cancer, have a close affinity with your changing moods; they are the best signs for flowing with your emotional shifts. Your opposite star sign, Taurus, an earth sign, is also not a bad balance with your deeply intense nature. They will anchor and secure you to the Earth, and somehow calm your extremes.

⊚ SCORPIO FRIEND ⊚

Scorpios enjoy a good level of friendship and usually have a diverse range of acquaintances, which they need to stimulate their intellectual and emotional interests.

For some people, having a Scorpio friend may be a little too intense. You're the sort of person that cuts straight to the chase, so to speak, diving into a person's character and emotional needs. In the first instance, this can be rather threatening to them. But you like to know exactly where you stand with others, and once you deem them to be worthy of your friendship, you do anything to support them and make sure they're looked after.

As a Scorpio friend, you are generous, hospitable and can be a lot of fun to be around. In fact, it's probably not a well-known fact that, although Scorpio is rather intense and serious, they do have the capacity to make others laugh, drawing on their past experiences and embellishing details to bring a great deal of joy to their associates.

With a Scorpio friend, you can rest assured your secrets are safe. They probably have many secrets of their own, so they understand the value of maintaining confidentiality. Furthermore, Scorpio is an excellent psychologist. If your secret rests on a certain problem you are experiencing, Scorpio is the best sign from which to get deep insights on how you can solve it or protect secrets.

Scorpio is not interested in one-off, light-hearted friendships or acquaintances. You prefer to deepen your connection with someone, especially if you feel as though you're compatible with them. I liken this to the concept of Japanese business relationships—in for the long haul!

Scorpios generally need to surround themselves with people who are interesting or have achieved or experienced something that makes them interesting to be around. Scorpios are never attracted to dull personalities, so if you fail to raise the level of interest of a Scorpio in your conversation, it means you need to go back to the drawing board to overhaul your character and bring something of value to the friendship. Otherwise, it's a no-go for Scorpio.

For those of you reading this wanting to know how best to develop a friendship with a Scorpio, you need to challenge them with outdoor activities, competitive sports or, at least, topics that may be new to them. Introduce them to new friends, take them out to unusual places that have a cultural or intellectual difference, and you'll win their hearts. They enjoy culture to a large extent: musical and cabaret shows, rock and even opera concerts appeal to them.

Loyal, as Long as You Reciprocate

Scorpios are extraordinarily loyal and dedicated in their friendships, and are proactive in making them work. But if they feel that others are not repaying the high level of energy that they're putting into the relationship, then they'll quickly withdraw and redirect those energies elsewhere.

⊚ SCORPIO ENEMY ⊚

Vengeance of a Scorpio

Scorpio is a formidable enemy, so beware. They may maintain a calm, cool exterior towards you— even if you are both aware they don't like you or they have chosen to become your adversary. But don't, for a moment, take this as an indication that all is fine and you're home and hosed. The Scorpio vengeance is second to none, and you will, at some point, have to contend with their wrath.

Scorpio, you're a very proud sign. If someone has crossed you or done the wrong thing by you, you feel as if it's a matter of honour that you set things right. In the process, you usually give others a good tongue lashing. But if the opportunity is not right, you will wait and wait and wait until the appropriate moment to take out your enemy.

Under these circumstances, the vengeful, obsessive and determined side of your nature brings out the worst in you. You, Scorpio, must learn how to deal with your adversaries in a much more wholesome manner, and in ways that don't undermine your own emotional, mental and physical wellbeing.

SCORPIO

AT HOME

THE ONLY WAY OF FINDING THE
LIMITS OF THE POSSIBLE IS BY
GOING BEYOND THEM INTO THE
IMPOSSIBLE.

Arthur C. Clarke

⊙ HOME FRONT ⊙

The secretive side of Scorpio is often found reflected in the way they live in and decorate their homes and living spaces.

Because you value privacy, Scorpio, and want to protect your loved ones, you'll normally guard your territory vehemently. Any outside intrusion is unwelcome, and even friends must give you some sort of forewarning before casually stopping off to say hi.

Scorpios have a love of luxury, and are known to be sensualists at heart. This is reflected in their choice of decor and furnishings, as well as the colour schemes that portray a rather sensual yet energising sort of atmosphere. Your colour choices will set the tone and mood to make people feel comfortable, but also alert and open to communication and mental or emotional stimulation.

CLEANLINESS IS CLOSE TO VIRGO-NESS

Scorpios are also obsessive, so you may keep your house spotlessly clean. Everything is usually neat and in order. In this way, you exhibit some Virgo traits. Even your books may be neatly arranged from tallest to shortest, and if this gets put out of order, you may start to feel uncomfortable.

Having possessions is a way that you measure your success, therefore objects of art such as paintings and unique furnishings are things on which you pride yourself. Your house will usually be a topic of discussion, but you also want your home environment to be warm and inviting.

Scorpios like to have a house that feels lived in—not clinical, cold or artistic simply for the sake of art. You like a functional environment, and one in which the furniture you have is practical and useful. You're born under the element of water, so even if you can't live by a lake or the ocean, having a pond or some type of fountain will give you the sense of being close to nature. A lush garden, which may have a place of sanctuary in the back where you can meditate and connect with yourself, is also a great idea.

You like to create a type of illusion in your home, and this is done with the use of exotic and passionate colours. Crimson, burgundy, maroon and other reds lend themselves to this. The darker colours, such as purple and black (a favourite of many Scorpios) and the darker blues, are also excellent choices for your home decor. Textures should be smooth and sleek, and the lighting should create a mystical—and maybe even dramatic—contrast from room to room.

You like furniture and fabrics that have a sensuousness about them. Leather furniture, raw materials and textures that are hard to the touch give you the sense that there's something unique and attractive about your furnishings. Once again, being born under a water sign, a fish tank may be a great accent in your home.

Scorpios love to entertain, to wine and dine with friends in the comfort of their abodes. With all the design aspects in keeping with your temperament, a night at your place will probably be one to remember.

KARMA, LUCK AND
MEDITATION ☙

Your motto is 'I Will'. Scorpio is one of the most determined star signs of the zodiac, and when you set yourself a challenge, you usually achieve it. This is because your ruling planets, Mars and Pluto, have indomitable will and give you the persistence to follow through.

In your last life, you developed a high degree of sensitivity and psychic insight. Cancer is the ninth sign from yours and indicates your caring and loving nature. This is why you are able to intuit so many things.

🪷 Future Karma

Your future karma is indicated by the sign of Pisces, the fifth sign from Scorpio. It is also the third water sign in the water trinity, telling us that you are moving towards a more unconditional way of loving. In your current stage of evolution, you are still somewhat preoccupied with sensuality, possession and power. Over time that will change.

Lucky Days

Mondays, Tuesdays, Thursdays and Sundays are lucky for your emotional healing and self-development. Spend a little time each day doing something spontaneous that you wouldn't normally do. This will augment your luck.

Lucky Numbers

Lucky numbers for Scorpio include the following. You may wish to experiment with these in lotteries and other games of chance:

9, 18, 27, 36, 45, 54

3, 12, 21, 30, 48, 57

2, 11, 20, 29, 38, 47, 56

Destiny Years

The most significant years in your life are likely to be 9, 18, 27, 36, 45, 54, 63, 72 and 81.

HEALTH, WELLBEING
☺ AND DIET ☺

Scorpio is the eighth sign of the zodiac, and governs such things as the urinary tract, sexual organs and organs of evacuation. That's why your star sign is closely aligned with these parts of your anatomy, and if something is to go wrong, these are the constitutionally weak parts of your body.

You have an incredibly intense way of living and sometimes overwork and play far too hard. This will ultimately impact on your body as a whole, but if, in particular, you're prone to drinking and smoking—which you're best to give up—the aforementioned areas are likely to be affected.

Some of the other areas with which you may experience health issues are the liver, the skin, and by virtue of being the sign opposite Taurus, which rules the throat, that part of your body as well.

Aries rules the head, and is in the sixth zone of health and disease from Scorpio. Some Scorpios suffer headaches based on tension or other suppressed emotions, and this can be a problem particularly in the early part of your life.

As a rule, you don't generally get slowed down by any illness or health issue because you have a very strong recuperative power. Your diet should, however, be rich in calcium, B-group vitamins and, of course, you should take supplements to strengthen the areas mentioned above.

Some of the fruits and vegetables with which you should supplement your diet include asparagus, cauliflower, onions, tomatoes and figs.

Great antioxidants are black cherries, wholegrains and seafood, along with green salads and copious amounts of nuts. These are excellent foods for maintaining your health and wellbeing.

❂ FINANCE FINESSE ❂

Money is extremely important to you, Scorpio, as shown by the fact that your Sun sign rules the eighth sign of the zodiac, which relates to shared money such as inheritances, joint investments, annuities and taxes.

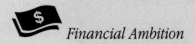

Financial Ambition

You're extremely focused on making money and, even from an early age, you tend to measure your success by the amount of cash you have in the bank. Symbols of luxury—such as prestigious cars, brand-name clothing, jewellery and other objects that reflect your success and ability to earn money—are part and parcel of your Scorpio nature.

The second sign to Scorpio is Sagittarius, which indicates the way that you earn your money and, to some extent, how you spend it. Jupiter, the ruler of Sagittarius, is magnanimous and very large. It shows you are able to earn large amounts of money, but are also very generous in the way you use it.

Most Scorpios are capable of earning high incomes, but I find that some of them are not fully able to capitalise on their talents until they are considerably older. This is because you don't compromise on what it is you want to do, and often those jobs are not that well paid until you've made a name for yourself, and acquired the reputation needed to demand a higher salary or fee for your services.

SCORPIO
AT WORK

WE ARE WHAT WE REPEATEDLY DO.
EXCELLENCE, THEREFORE, IS NOT AN
ACT, BUT A HABIT.

Aristotle

⊚ SCORPIO CAREER ⊚

IDEAL PROFESSIONS

Insurance agent

Banker or market analyst

Stockbroker or investor

Astrologer

Psychologist

Forensic investigator

You are a tireless worker, Scorpio, and sometimes one wonders where you get the energy to keep going. This is particularly evident with Scorpio mums, who not only hold down full-time jobs but are just as capable of managing a house, their husbands' needs and those of the children and other family members as well. This powerful energy is granted by the distant planet, Pluto, one of the two rulers of your Sun sign.

Scorpio is primarily concerned with excellent work, and if someone should hinder that, a Scorpio's anger knows no bounds. But generally, even if there is a tense situation or problem, Scorpio is rather cool under the circumstances and takes full control, even if he or she is not the boss.

You are intense and passionate about your work, but unless you have a love of what you do, you're not likely to stick with a particular job for too long. You have a belief that loving the work you do is somehow part of the universal process in providing you the success and satisfaction you expect from it.

You have an immense ability to focus and concentrate on tasks—much to the amazement of others. You don't stop your work until you've sorted out a problem or achieved the desired end. You also don't need someone standing over you, breathing down your neck or lashing you with a whip to get the job done.

You take the initiative and complete whatever tasks are expected of you. In this way, you are a responsible worker, and gain the respect of colleagues, employers and clients alike.

You have a great deal of confidence, but this is not simply because you are cocky or egotistical (although some Scorpios are). You gained this confidence through systematically learning your craft or trade, and by applying the principles you learned, together with your life experiences, which also add to your arsenal of skilful abilities.

 **The Sun**

Your workplace planet is the Sun. What does this mean to you professionally? Because the Sun is bright and warm, you are likely to be successful and shine in your chosen line of work. Leo is the sign ruled by the Sun and indicates your ability to win the adulation of others.

Mars

Mars is Scorpio's career ruler. Mars makes you impulsive in action and a tireless worker. Few can keep up with you. Learn to moderate your work practices and the hours you keep at the office. This will support your health and also your personal relationships. Many Scorpios are workaholics.

Those who work with you should understand that you're a very honest person, and that you expect the same truthfulness in return.

Scorpios do well at criminology, police work and psychic sciences and practices. Other suitable professions include insurance, banking, psychiatry, psychology, research and any sort of scientific activity. You also love the power of money, so professions involving lots of it may suit you well.

☺ SCORPIO BOSS ☺

Being born under Scorpio, you are a loyalty freak! Nothing is more important, in your estimation, than business partners or employees who are prepared to dedicate themselves to your vision and goals, and to loyally stand by you.

This sounds like a tall order, but those on the receiving end of your kindness and reciprocated loyalty realise that by committing themselves to you, they have a very powerful ally who will stand by them in the most difficult times.

Scorpio people and, in particular, bosses, are extremely competitive and hate to lose. This is why they are so successful. And as long as you maintain an honourable approach to your business dealings, you can be as competitive as you like. You work hard, and demand superhuman results from yourself and from those you draw into your circle for your career objectives.

Your enthusiasm and dedication are contagious, and your clients always feel as if they receive the best possible service from you. You expect this high standard of service from those you employ, too.

Unfortunately, you are not the most trusting person, and until someone has proven themselves to you, they tend to feel as if you are judging them harshly. You have a reason for doing this, however, and that is to detect the weaknesses or shortcomings these people possess in order to help them become better.

You love a well-ordered company and expect everyone to know their rightful place. Timing, punctuality and positive workplace relations are key factors in helping you feel secure and motivated to do your job without having to worry about everything around you.

Because Pluto is one of your ruling planets, you'll want to control everyone and everything in your orb. That's possible to do, but unless you are able to delegate tasks, you'll end up alienating others and not really achieving the level of success that you would otherwise reach.

SCORPIO
◎ EMPLOYEE ◎

 Efficient Employee

You are a highly motivated person, so when it comes to any type of work, you are generally capable enough to know what's expected of you, and to do your work in a skilful and timely manner. You are also punctual, you like to maintain an orderly approach to your tasks, and you have a way of developing systems that makes you highly efficient. In fact, you are more efficient than many of the people around you.

You are the type of person who sets objectives—short-, medium- and long-term goals—by which to measure success.

Being tenacious, you hate to waste time, and don't like to get too involved in the social gossip that may be part of your workplace environment. Your objectivity can put others' noses out of joint, but this doesn't bother you because you are totally focused on achieving your aims.

You are disliked by those who see your high output as a threat to their easygoing and possibly lazy natures. For this reason, it's sometimes best for you to hide your talents and not always show what you're capable of. In this way, you won't create too many enemies around you.

You are fearless, inventive and are not scared to take a risk. Courage is one of your greatest assets, and therefore, unlike most, you're not scared to move somewhere else if your current situation does not satisfy you or you feel as if it's a dead-end for your overall career objectives.

WORK LOYALTY

Just as I mentioned that loyalty is at the heart of the Scorpio boss, you, too, as a Scorpio employee, are extremely loyal. If a situation offers you the right sort of growth path for your career, you'll stand by your employers and colleagues.

Money is an extremely important aspect of your work, and you tend to measure your success by the cash that you acquire. You have a brilliant mind, and coupled with your shrewd, logical and intuitive sense, you are an incredibly gifted worker—employers are quick to note this.

With work colleagues, you demand respect, and you are quick to retaliate if someone insults you or questions your ability or, more importantly, your integrity. If you perceive an injustice, you are likely to step up to the plate and voice your opposition, even if this means provoking an adverse reaction. You are certainly a person of high principles.

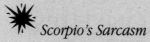

Scorpio's Sarcasm

A Scorpio loves researching and doing a job well.
They are also independent and take the initiative in
work. Don't obstruct them, however, or you could
risk their sarcastic vengeance.

PROFESSIONAL RELATIONSHIPS: BEST AND WORST

BEST PAIRING:
SCORPIO AND SAGITTARIUS

This is an excellent relationship as far as business is concerned. Scorpio and Sagittarius are ruled by planets that are considered bosom buddies by astrologers. Sagittarius also happens to fall in the finance sector of Scorpio, meaning that the Jupiter-ruled sign offers you a real opportunity to make great profits by increasing your income stream.

What you really love about your Sagittarian business partner are their broad views and open-mindedness when it comes to expanding your business interests. Actually, you may find that they are a little too open and carefree, which could make you feel a bit nervous. Trust is going to be an important element in allowing Sagittarius to move forward in your best interests. As long as you keep a tight rein on the monetary situation, you can rest assured that, at least on mental and emotional levels, the two of you will get on very well.

Most Sagittarians I have had the pleasure of being involved with are very optimistic, free-thinking and original in the way they approach business. You mustn't dominate them if you want to bring out their best. I also like the fact that you are a deep thinker, and for the most part, Scorpios are excellent at managing money, so the two of you balance each other very well.

Sagittarians need a great deal of variety, freedom and independence in executing their duties in their professional lives. If you can afford them this little luxury, they will perform much better, and the end result will be an increased reputation and more money in everyone's pockets.

Sagittarius is open and honest in all their dealings, and if there is a fault in their personality, it could be that they are often too generous with money. You may need to correct them on this matter, and advise them that trusting others too quickly could be a mistake. Once you agree on the parameters of your association, you'll both function extremely well in each other's company, supporting the other to do their best.

I consider the Scorpio-Sagittarius business association one of the best, if not *the* best, in the zodiac. Of course, some of the other water signs also fare well with you, but for the sheer opportunity to earn money, I believe Sagittarius is a sign with whom you can't go wrong.

WORST PAIRING: SCORPIO AND TAURUS

Taurus is a fixed zodiac sign just like your own. For this reason you both become stuck in your ways. This is why Taurus to you has some real issues in moving forward especially with issues of money. Being tight fisted in your opinion, can make dealing with Taurus a nightmare. You will feel justified in your expenses only to find that your Taurus partner will be forever questioning you on the whys and wherefores of your spending.

You consider yourself progressive in thought, and action and I are always looking for new avenues to enhances and grow your business. With Taurus, the tried and tested is a much more palatable option and this is where you're also both find yourself in head on confrontation on numerous occasions. When trying to explain your reasoning, you will always feel as if you justifying your ideas. Eventually you'll feel as if you're bang your head against a wall my to convince Taurus of the benefits that might occur if they were to simply open their minds a little more.

Once you involve yourself in a relationship with them however, you may have difficulty getting out of this arrangement. Because you admire their tenacity, loyalty and ability to do things properly, you will find yourself constantly balancing these two extremes. This will cause immense frustration. You have a strong sense of loyalty as well and it is for this reason that you will feel guilty even thinking about severing the ties but don't forget that the frustration will be mutual.

Power and control are the key words in your partnership. Either or both of you will eventually try to dominate the other and this will start a never ending cycle of dispute and mistrust. Although many astrologers consider this an excellent partnership, and yes that may be the case in certain contexts such as friendship, or romantic association, it imperative that you think carefully about becoming involved with Taurus financially.

Because communication is essential in any relationship including business, when the going gets tough for the two of you, it's likely you will both need to deal with what I call "shutdown mode". This will be a disaster as things need to be talked about and when the two of you disconnect, nothing will get done. You'll both dig your heels in and at some point when you've both had enough an explosive and acrimonious end may be predicted for this match.

If you feel a business arrangement with a Taurus partner is unavoidable, my suggestion is that you have clearly defined terms of our agreement with mutually acceptable exit clauses.

SCORPIO
IN LOVE

WE WERE GIVEN: TWO HANDS TO
HOLD, TWO LEGS TO WALK, TWO
EYES TO SEE AND TWO EARS TO
LISTEN. BUT WHY ONLY ONE HEART?
BECAUSE THE OTHER HEART WAS
GIVEN TO SOMEONE ELSE—FOR US
TO FIND.

Anonymous

ROMANTIC
⊚ COMPATIBILITY ⊚

How compatible are you with your current partner, lover or friend? Did you know that astrology can reveal a whole new level of understanding between people, simply by looking at their star sign and that of their partner? I'd like to share some special insights that will help you better appreciate your strengths and challenges using Sun sign compatibility.

The Sun reflects your drive, willpower and personality. The essential qualities of two star signs blend like two pure colours that produce an entirely new colour. Relationships, similarly, produce their own emotional colours when two people interact. The following section is a general guide to your romantic prospects with others and how, by knowing the astrological 'colour' of each other, the art of love can help you create a masterpiece.

Each of the twelve star signs has a greater or lesser affinity with the others. The two quick-reference tables will show you who's hot and who's not as far as your relationships are concerned.

The Star Sign Compatibility table rates your chance as a percentage of general compatibility, while the Horoscope Compatibility table summarises the reasons why. The results of each star sign combination are also listed.

When reading I ask you to remember that no two star signs are ever *totally* incompatible. With effort and compromise, even the most difficult astrological matches can work. Don't close your mind to the full range of life's possibilities! Learning about each other and ourselves is the most important facet of astrology.

Good luck in your search for love, and may the stars shine upon you in 2012!

STAR SIGN COMPATIBILITY
FOR LOVE AND FRIENDSHIP
(PERCENTAGES)

	Aries	Taurus	Gemini	Cancer	Leo	Virgo	Libra	Scorpio	Sagittarius	Capricorn	Aquarius	Pisces
Aries	60	65	65	65	90	45	70	80	90	50	55	65
Taurus	60	70	70	80	70	90	75	85	50	95	80	85
Gemini	70	70	75	60	80	75	90	60	75	50	90	50
Cancer	65	80	60	75	70	75	60	95	55	45	70	90
Leo	90	70	80	70	85	75	65	75	95	45	70	75
Virgo	45	90	75	75	75	70	80	85	70	95	50	70
Libra	70	75	90	60	65	80	80	85	80	85	95	50
Scorpio	80	85	60	95	75	85	85	90	80	65	60	95
Sagittarius	90	50	75	55	95	70	80	85	85	55	60	75
Capricorn	50	95	50	45	45	95	85	65	55	85	70	85
Aquarius	55	80	90	70	70	50	95	60	60	70	80	55
Pisces	65	85	50	90	75	70	50	95	75	85	55	80

In the compatibility table above please note that some compatibilities have seemingly contradictory ratings. Why you ask? Well, remember that no two people experience the relationship in exactly the same way. For one person a relationship may be more advantageous, more supportive than for the other. Sometimes one gains more than the other partner and therefore the compatibility rating will be higher for them.

HOROSCOPE COMPATIBILITY
⊙ FOR SCORPIO ⊙

Scorpio with		Romance/Sexual
Aries		Sexuality will dominate your time together, and Aries will boost your desire to explore new possibilities
Taurus		You'll feel excited by Taurus, a powerful attraction
Gemini		Sexually you'll fascinate Gemini, but they might feel as if you're trying to dominate and control their emotions

	Friendship		Professional
✔	Strong emotional and karmic connections create a great friendship	✘	You will be at loggerheads because you are both very determined and forceful in your views—you'll clash intensely
✘	Brings up psychological challenges in the area of power and control	✘	Before getting too involved with them, make sure you clearly understand their financial needs
✘	Your planets don't easily get on with each other, and this may eventually create uneasiness in your friendship	✘	A fine blend of Scorpio determination and Gemini flair is possible, but they are too scattered for your liking

Scorpio with		Romance/Sexual
Cancer		Good match, but you are driven by the sexual aspects of a relationship and need more passion than Cancer can provide
Leo		You both need to feel respected by each other if you're going to make a go of this relationship—exciting!
Virgo		You're sometimes insensitive and don't take Virgo's basic emotional needs into account; great chemistry, though
Libra		You'll be attracted to sensual Libra, and they'll react nicely to your hot-blooded temperament

Friendship	Professional
✔ You can kick up your heels and let down your guard with them	✔ Curb your desire to dominate sensitive Cancer with your unrealistic demands and this could work
✔ Mutual respect makes this a great friendship	✔ Many of your life lessons will be tied up in your financial relationship with them
✔ Common interests indicate a fun friendship—unless Virgo becomes too critical of you	✔ This is usually a very practical and efficient partnership that can make both Scorpio and Virgo happy
✔ Libra encourages you and you'll be prepared to share your emotional and social self with them	✔ Libra will ignite you, and can send your mind down new avenues

Scorpio with		Romance/Sexual
Scorpio		You both love deeply, but are possessive, jealous and suspicious of each other, which could eventually stifle you
Sagittarius		This is a dynamic combination, but it shouldn't be taken for granted: inspire each other!
Capricorn		You might overwhelm Capricorn with your enthusiasm and hot passion, so go slowly
Aquarius		Good communication in the bedroom will be absolutely essential if you are to bring out this air sign's passionate side

Friendship	Professional
✔ Another Scorpio instinctively understands your mind and heart, you easily share your secrets with them	✔ You both work intensely with the same objectives so this can be a successful union
✔ Scorpio and Sagittarius can be great friends; their ruling planets are friendly	✔ Your financial relationship can be excessive; unless Sagittarius sticks to basic ground rules, the partnership may fail
✔ Friendship and a great social life are on the cards with Capricorns	✔ Both of you are industrious, hardworking and determined, and you're both committed to achieving your goals
✘ They won't stand for someone who is intellectually lazy—you will need to be forward-thinking and open to new ideas	✘ Not the best combination for business success, but Aquarius offers novel enterprises to you

Pisces

Extremes in passion
are likely between
you, but this is a
near-perfect match

Friendship	Professional
✔ Pisces understands your complex personality and knows how to touch your body, mind and spirit	✗ Their compassionate and idealistic personalities are not considered right for business by you

SCORPIO
◎ PARTNERSHIPS ◎

 Scorpio + Aries

Power and control dominate the relationship when a Scorpio and Aries combine forces. How you use these will determine how much happiness you both experience. In many cases, a battle of wills is likely, because Aries has just as much fire and determination as you. Be prepared for a romance of equality.

 Scorpio + Taurus

Your constant need to express yourself through sex will flatter Taurus at first, but they need more affection, sensitivity and warmth if they are to feel secure about the relationship lasting. Taurus is very touchy-feely by nature, but they don't want just sex! They need to feel secure.

 Scorpio + Gemini

As a couple, you two will have to prepare yourselves for some pretty intense times. Gemini is light-hearted, frivolous and intellectual, and will meet you head to head when it comes to communication. But your communication styles are different: you prefer in-depth discussions about one subject, while Gemini likes to keep it light and breezy and talk about a multitude of things.

Scorpio + Cancer

Although Scorpio and Cancer are well suited elementally, there are differences sexually. You are driven by the purely sensual and sexual aspects of a relationship. You need much more passion in your romance than Cancer does. Cancer needs love and bonding before they can express unbridled passion.

 Scorpio + Leo

You're both stubborn and have fixed opinions about things, but your spirit will thaw under Leo's warm rays of sunshine. You're sensual, emotional and, for the most part, an intense person. This is exactly the type of energy that will attract Leo and create a powerful emotional relationship.

 Scorpio + Virgo

There are many Scorpios and Virgos who've been attracted to each other. And lots of them have been able to create happy, comfortable and fulfilling lives by pooling their financial, mental and emotional resources. This is usually a very practical and efficient partnership that can make both of you happy.

Scorpio + Libra

Your overprotective and jealous streak is something Librans are not able to accept easily; at some point, even if you think they're dealing with it, you'll be in for a rude awakening. They need to dig deep into their arsenal of diplomatic weaponry to get around your bossiness and inflexibility.

Scorpio + Scorpio

Relationships between two Scorpios are not what other star signs would consider idyllic, because there are often tremendous upheavals and mood swings due to both sides' inflexible position on many issues. If either of you is incapable of loving the other unconditionally, these problems will not be easy to overcome.

Scorpio + Sagittarius

Because Sagittarius likes to share, your sex life can be exciting, but it could be one-sided until you become trusting and open with them. When you come out from behind your wall of reservedness, Sagittarius will find your loving responses irresistible.

Scorpio + Capricorn

Your sexual compatibility starts off slowly, because your ruling planets are very different to each other. You are outgoing in terms of sexual expression, while Capricorn is more reserved. You might overwhelm Capricorn with your enthusiasm and fiery passion, however.

 Scorpio + Aquarius

You're both determined, and you stick at whatever you take on until it's finished. Also, you aren't afraid of challenges. This is usually essential in terms of a relationship's durability, but in this case, it may be the opposite: the more you dig in your heels, the less chance that it will work.

 Scorpio + Pisces

When Pisces and Scorpio fall for each other, Scorpio is often able to soothe the emotional storms of a Pisces' inner life, and help them put aside their conflicts or mental pain. Pisces will be good at using their compassion to manage your intense and sometimes sarcastic approaches.

PLATONIC
RELATIONSHIPS:
BEST AND WORST

BEST PAIRING:
SCORPIO AND VIRGO

There are many Scorpios and Virgos who've been attracted to each other and subsequently develop a great friendship and social connection. Many of them have been able to create a happy, comfortable and fulfilling life by pooling their intellectual, social and emotional resources. This is usually a very practical and efficient connection that can make both Scorpio and Virgo satisfied in each other's company.

Your ruling planet, Pluto, is challenging—and challenging in a most confrontational way—whereas Virgo prefers to do battle rationally and in a way that is courteous and unassuming. You are brutally honest, and can lack the tact and diplomacy that Virgo needs. However, Virgo is able to cope with your tough attitude and eventually you will respect them for this.

In a permanent liaison they'll feel that you're insensitive: your blunt manner shows a lack of respect and you don't take their basic emotional needs into account. And you'll become irritated, if not completely frustrated, by their overly logical examination of every minor issue. Strangely, though, these apparent negatives work to finetune your characters, and slowly but surely you get along.

Often, you'll feel as if you're being monitored and tested against Virgo's standards. They won't openly judge you, but you'll certainly feel that what you do and say is forever being scrutinised. This will cause you to improve yourself and become a better person.

You will develop some talents you may previously have been unaware of because of your friendship with Virgo. Lighten up and you'll feel much more confident about your relationship, making it an excellent match.

Virgo offers you emotional and intellectual security. The two of you can also work towards financial stability, and build a mutual support system that gives you more than the basic emotional or social fulfilment of most friendships, because you have some prosperity thrown in for good measure.

Be wary, however. Mercury, which co-rules Virgo, is opposite in nature to you, so think twice before taking the friendship to any serious sexual level. Virgos are more ideally suited to long-term friendships with you. This is because Jupiter, which has a bearing on your romantic life, and is a thoroughly lucky planet for you, also has a bearing on their destiny. You'll feel attracted to them, and will want to have them in your life.

WORST PAIRING:
SCORPIO AND ARIES

Power and control is the name of the game when a Scorpio and Aries combine forces. How you use these will determine how much happiness you have together. In many cases, a battle of wills is likely, because Aries have just as much fire and purposefulness as you. Be prepared for a clash of wills with your Aries friend.

And, of course, when your elements are blended, you have fire and water together, which creates heat and steam. The water of Scorpio and fire of Aries can, in fact, be quite a sizzling combination once it gets going, but remember that water puts out fire. You will immediately be attracted to the excitement and energy of each other, but don't ever dampen the spirit of an Aries—they won't stand for it. Come to think of it, neither will you if they try to exert control!

You will excite the hot-headed Aries, and they will boost your desire to explore new possibilities. You're both strong-willed individuals with unique personalities, so compromise will be important if you are to make a go of it. I'm not sure if either of you will make the necessary concessions to the other, though. Aries will find it hard to negotiate and come to an understanding with you.

You are a very secretive and private person, whereas Aries is pretty outspoken on most matters. Your styles are quite different and communication is an arena that is likely to create conflicts between you. You will be at loggerheads over life perspectives, too, because you are both determined and forceful in your views. You'll clash intensely. These bouts of rage, when you both attempt to prove your superiority, will cause you to infuriate each other constantly!

You become terribly exasperated when your Aries friend tries to assert their correctness on most topics, knowing full well they just don't have the knowledge they are pretending to. I can see you throwing your arms up in frustration and walking away from this friendship, Scorpio.

....

TOO MUCH COMPETITIVENESS

Aries will attempt to dominate you in your social sphere, which will seriously annoy you. You'll feel as if you are constantly trying to one-up them in most situations. This could be a disastrous combination if you don't like submitting yourself to someone else— and most Scorpios don't. Learning the art of humility will be your most important lesson with these Aries folk.

....

SEXUAL RELATIONSHIPS: BEST AND WORST

BEST PAIRING: SCORPIO AND PISCES

What can I say except that a combination of Scorpio and Pisces is a truly magical love match? Some may even go so far as to call it a match made in heaven. The reason for this is that your planets are extremely friendly, and your star signs are in a favourable triangular position to each other.

You both have a combination of sensitive emotional energies that create a natural attraction between you, and you have the added benefit of possessing powerful psychic vibrations that lead you to understand each other without words. This shows that you are most definitely karmically connected.

Pisces seems to understand intuitively just how your complex personality operates, and you have a sense of what you need to do to protect them and make them comfortable and secure in your presence. Usually, when a Scorpio and a Pisces meet, they fall head over heels in love with each other. If you're already in a relationship with a Pisces, you'll understand what I'm saying.

Pisces sometimes lives in the realm of the spirit, with their head in the clouds and with little connection to what's going on around them. Very few star signs—except, of course, you, Scorpio—have the ability to anchor them and manage their somewhat detached manner. You're able to soothe and calm the emotional storms, as well as the somewhat changeable moods of your Pisces partner. In return, they do the same for you, because you are also often overwhelmed by your feelings.

> *If, as a Scorpio, you were to fall in love with a Piscean,*
> *you'd realise immediately just how lucky you are.*
> *The appreciation you have for each other is a very*
> *important aspect of what makes this relationship just*
> *so special.*

There is also an extraordinarily positive sexual relationship that can be expected between the two of you, too. Many Scorpio-Pisces relationships go the distance because this match is excellent on many levels.

WORST PAIRING:
SCORPIO AND GEMINI

As a couple, you will have to prepare yourselves for some pretty intense times. Gemini is light-hearted, playful and logical, and will meet you head to head when it comes to communication. But your communication styles aren't able to be synchronised: you prefer in-depth discussions about one subject, while Gemini likes to keep the conversation light and breezy and talk about a multitude of things. Sometimes you feel a little weary of all of their talk, and simply want to get down to some raunchy fun!

Your planets don't easily get along, and this will eventually create uneasiness in your romance. If you are patient with Gemini, however, they may come to realise that your probing mind can reveal the deeper side of their intelligence, and this will lead to their personal growth. But Gemini hates waiting around and is likely to look to greener pastures well before you can develop any sort of genuine sexual compatibility.

Scorpios know how hard it is to be committed in a relationship—they are so choosy in selecting a partner who has to fit into their very busy lifestyles. They also demand undying loyalty, passion and intellectual stimulation.

QUIZ:
HAVE YOU FOUND YOUR PERFECT
⊚ MATCH? ⊚

Do you dare take the following quiz to see just how good a lover you are? Remember, although the truth sometimes hurts, it's the only way to develop your relationship skills.

We are all searching for our soulmate: that idyllic romantic partner who will fulfil our wildest dreams of love and emotional security. Unfortunately, finding true love isn't easy. Sometimes, even when you are in a relationship, you can't help but wonder whether or not your partner is right for you. How can you possibly know?

It's essential to question your relationships and to work on ways that will improve your communication and overall happiness with your partner. It's also a good idea, when meeting someone new, to study their intentions and read between the lines. In the first instance, when your hormones are taking over, it's easy to get carried away and forget some of the basic principles of what makes for a great relationship that is going to endure.

You're probably wondering where to start. Are you in a relationship currently? Are you looking for love, but finding it difficult to choose between two or more people? Are you simply not able to meet someone? Well, there are some basic questions you can ask yourself to discover the truth of just how well suited you and your partner are for each other. If you don't have a partner at the moment, you might like to reflect on your previous relationships to improve your chances next time round.

The following quiz is a serious attempt to take an honest look at yourself and see whether or not your relationships are on track. Don't rush through the questionnaire, but think carefully about your practical day-to-day life and whether or not the relationship you are in genuinely fulfils your needs and the other person's needs. There's no point being in a relationship if you're gaining no satisfaction out of it.

Now, if you aren't completely satisfied with the results you get, don't give up! It's an opportunity for you to work at the relationship and to improve things. But you mustn't let your ego get in the road, because that's not going to get you anywhere.

So here's a checklist for you, Scorpio, to see if he or she is the right one for you.

Scoring System:

Yes = 1 point

No = 0 points

❷ Is your partner perceptive enough to know what's on your mind without you telling them?

❷ Is he or she a Pisces, Taurus, Cancer, Virgo or Capricorn?

❷ Is he or she strong enough to maintain a tempestuous lifestyle?

❷ Are they interesting enough to remain challengingly enigmatic?

❷ Are they loyal and faithful to you?

❷ Do you feel content and happy around them?

❷ Are you always excited by them, even after being with them for a long time?

❷ Do they give you the full attention and care that you need?

❷ Are they fair to you?

❷ Do they listen to you, and give you an honest opinion?

❷ Do they understand and accept you for who you are?

❷ Can your partner cope with your intensity?

❷ Does he or she give you time and space when you need to be alone?

❷ Do they respect your belongings, and would never do anything with your possessions without your knowing?

❷ Do you realise that you are now not attracted to anyone else anymore—just to your partner?

Have you jotted down your answers honestly? If you're finding it hard to come up with the correct answers, let your intuition help and try not to force them. Of course, there's no point pretending and turning a blind eye to treatment that is less than acceptable, otherwise you're not going to have a realistic appraisal of your prospects with your current love interest. Here are the possible points you can score.

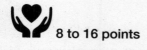 **8 to 16 points**

A good match. This shows you've obviously done something right, and that the partner you have understands you and is able to reciprocate in just the way you need. But this doesn't mean you should become lazy and not continue working on your relationship. There's always room to improve and make your already excellent relationship even better.

 5 to 7 points

Half-hearted prospect. You're going to need to work hard at your relationship, and this will require a close self-examination of just who may be at fault. You know, it takes two to tango and it's more than likely a combination of both your attitudes is what is dragging down your relationship. Systematically go over each of the above questions and try to make a list of where you can improve. I guarantee that your relationship will improve if given some time and sincerity on your part. If, after a genuine effort of working at it, you find things still haven't improved, it may be time for you to rethink your future with this person.

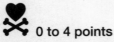 **0 to 4 points**

On the rocks. I'm sorry to say that this relationship is not founded on a sufficiently strong enough base of mutual respect and understanding. It's likely that the two of you argue a lot, don't see eye to eye or, frankly, have completely different ideas of what sort of lifestyle and emotional needs you each have. The big question here is why are you still with this person?

Again, this requires some honest self-examination to see if there is some inherent insecurity which is causing you to hold on to something that has outgrown its use in your life. Old habits die hard, as they say, and you may also fear letting go of a relationship that you have become accustomed to, even though it doesn't fulfil your needs. Self-honesty is the key here. At certain times in life you may need to make some rather big sacrifices to move on to a new phase, which will then hopefully attract the right sort of partner to you.

2012
YEARLY OVERVIEW

A FAILURE IS A MAN WHO HAS
BLUNDERED BUT IS NOT ABLE TO
CASH IN ON THE EXPERIENCE.

Elbert Hubbard

⊚ KEY EXPERIENCES ⊚

The year 2012 is a key time for Scorpios, and the approaching Saturn transit in your Sun sign for the first time in almost 30 years is an important development in your life after October. Until that time, however, many of your past experiences will continue to be digested and analysed. The effort of making sense of them will set you up for a new and exciting cycle in the years to come.

Mercury brings with it a strong sense of professional purpose, and for those of you who struggle to find meaning in your careers, your communication, learning and considerable soul searching will bring you some resolution in this area as well.

One of the key months of the year will be February, when Jupiter influences your relationship sector, bringing with it renewed optimism for your most intimate relationships.

In June, the spiritual planet Neptune activates your desire to understand your true nature and to bring out the compassionate side of your personality. You will be helping others at this time, and, in the process will be helping yourself as well.

August is a powerful period for your professional activities, with Mars bringing with it a high degree of energy. But please be careful, because impatience goes hand in glove with some of the assertive elements of this transit. After September the 17th, you will experience a similar effect due to the continuing Martian presence.

October and November are powerful transits that conclude the year, and Saturn conjoining your Sun sign brings with it an increased level of responsibility.

ROMANCE AND
◉ FRIENDSHIP ◉

This year, you have every opportunity to make a go of your relationships, because the important and beneficial planet Jupiter transits your zone of marriage rather quickly in the next few months. In fact, its decisive action means that in approximately seven months it will activate, nourish and expand your relationships, doing what normally takes a year. So, Scorpio, get ready for some exciting times ahead!

Venus enters your zone of romance around the 14th of January, so you will be expressing yourself most joyfully at this time. If you are not in a permanent relationship, you could find yourself in a positive situation with someone who is likely to excite you on every level of your being.

In February, Neptune enters this same zone of romance, indicating that your highest ideals are likely to come to fruition.

One point I should mention, however, is that Saturn, the serious and sobering planet of the solar system, is hovering just behind your Sun sign, and when it makes its entry into Scorpio in late October, things might cool off a little bit. Try to keep a level head and don't expect too much too soon. Patience is a virtue, and that will be certainly one of the main lessons for you, especially in the latter part of 2012.

All in all, this should be a time for you to fulfil your dreams and, if you are currently in a relationship, you can look forward to a period of renewed love, participation in shared activities, and a new level of awareness that will satisfy you and your partner fully.

 Relationships on the Rise

When the planets move around your horoscope, there are certain times when you will be more fortunate in meeting and connecting with those people who can fulfil you on an emotional level.

Some of the key dates earlier in the year include the period from the 8th to the 14th of January, when Mercury and Venus offer you excellent communication, quick learning, and an abundance of interesting if not sensually uplifting discussions.

ATTRACTIVE AND SOCIAL IN FEBRUARY

When Venus aspects Scorpio around the 2nd of February, you can look forward to a new friendship and some love heading your way. You will take a great deal of pleasure in joining your friends in many new activities, which has much to do with your sexual and physical appeal as well. You'll be far more attractive at this time, and will also be aware of just how beautiful you really are. Others will note this too, so you can expect a great deal of flattery from those around you.

Around the same time, Neptune, the planet of spiritual ideals and heightened creativity, touches on your zone of love and creative enterprises. You may find that there is some confusion surrounding the relationships you have been in, so take care not to rush into things.

In the first week of March, especially around the 5th, Venus moves through your zone of marriage, so your one-on-one relationships will be highlighted at this time. This should bring a period of peace, especially for those who have been undergoing some rather hard times.

Between the 1st and the 4th of April, sexual and sensual episodes are high on the agenda, and you will attract others very easily. A person you could become sexually involved with could act as the catalyst for a transformation at the deepest level of your being. This is an important transit for intimacy.

DEEPENING FRIENDSHIPS IN SEPTEMBER

Friendships in particular take a turn for the better after the 1st of September. At this time, you will find yourself experiencing a greater and even deeper degree of communication with friends than you have in the past. Sharing your thoughts and ideas with others will come easily, and this is a time when your mutual interests could centre around education, learning new ideas, and even revealing intimate secrets on how you can improve your relationships.

Venus moves in the upper part of your horoscope after the 5th of September. You will find that your relationships and work will blend excellently at this time. You will be interested to know more about those with whom you work, and this could create closer relationships with people who have previously been only work colleagues.

In the final part of the year, particularly when Venus enters your Sun sign after the 22nd of November, you will, once again, want to express your deepest feelings to someone close to you. If that person is not receptive, it will create some frustration, but generally, this is an excellent time when harmony should prevail in most of your relationships, both intimate and social.

⊚ WORK AND MONEY ⊚

 Harness Your Moneymaking Powers

Making money can be summed up in an equation:

$$m\text{ (\$ money)} = e\text{ (energy)} \times t\text{ (time)} \times l\text{ (love)}$$

If one of the above factors is not present—for example, energy or love—you could still make money, but you won't be ideally fulfilled in the process.

It's absolutely essential to understand the universal laws of attraction and success when speaking about money. It is also necessary to understand that when you love what you do, you infuse your work with the qualities of attention, love and perfection.

With these qualities, you endow your work with a sort of electromagnetic appeal: a power that draws people to your work and causes them to appreciate what you do. This, in turn, generates a desire for people to use your services, buy your products and respect you for the great work you perform. This will without a doubt elevate you to higher and higher positions because you will be regarded as someone who exercises great diligence and skill in your actions.

As a determined individual, Scorpio, it is important for you to earn money to display what a hard worker you are and just how committed you are to the tasks you set yourself. The year 2012 is no different. In fact, you will want to ramp up your energy levels, as shown by the key position of one of your ruling planets, Mars, in your zone of profitability, Virgo, as the year commences.

You are driven to increase your profitability, and this can be done through networking with those who have good connections and are prepared to help you, knowing that you are an excellent worker and a loyal employee. This year, loyalty and team effort are two of the secrets of your success.

You mustn't allow Saturn to prevent you from getting out and putting your best foot forward. As well as Jupiter positing your zone of public relations in the early part of the year, there is every likelihood you will be in one of the best positions yet to create new partnerships, acquire fresh customers, and expand your professional business activities in 2012.

Your career planet, the Sun, transits your zone of speculation after the 19th of February. This is a good opportunity for Scorpios to play their hand by investing in stocks, bonds and other markets. You should gain considerably at this time but, as with all things, if you are not an expert, then proceed cautiously.

MIND, BODY, WALLET

To tap into your moneymaking powers during the coming twelve months, you must also guard against health issues that may undermine your efforts. After the 20th of March, you may need to learn a few lessons about slowing down, because you could be ignoring some of your body signals. They may continue up until the end of May.

If you are careful to watch your diet, get adequate sleep and be patient in achieving your goals, you can achieve excellent results in the second half of the year. When Jupiter aspects your career sector after the 3rd of June, you may have the opportunity to improve some of elements of your career. Of course, building up your skill set is one of most obvious ways of generating more income. That is certainly the case this year.

Jupiter also moves into your zone of shared resources after the 12th of June. Don't make too many big plans just now; if necessary, try to get others involved in what you are doing. Better planning is essential, and to do this, you may need to talk to your accountant, investment or superannuation advisor, and your lawyer. Inheritances could come your way or you might be in a position where you need to draw up a will. In either case, you will need to think about these sorts of things.

From August to October, you will have the perfect opportunity to connect with friends who have the skills I mentioned earlier to help you forge ahead in your professional efforts. With Mars entering your zone of finances around the 7th of October, be careful not to fight about money, or be too demanding with the ones you love. You need their help, too, because no man or woman is an island onto themselves.

From October to December, spend some time grooming yourself and looking your best, especially if you are dealing with the public or going to meetings. First impressions, if they're good enough, will be something you can use to hone those moneymaking powers of yours in the coming months.

 Tips for Financial Success

I have already mentioned how to tap into your moneymaking powers, but you should expect to earn more and make a greater impression on others this year. There are some additional dates that will help you take full advantage of what is likely to come your way in 2012. You must capitalise on these opportunities — they can be few and far between.

Some of the key dates when the planets are in favourable aspect to your Sun sign or financial planets are the 13th and the 18th of March, and the 20th of April.

CONTRACT HIGHLIGHTS

Additional dates in the middle of the year are the 19th of May, the 3rd of June and the 21st of June. Around these times, you may need to look at contracts, legal issues or other bureaucratic points which, if you are unaware of, may hamstring you down the track. Broaden your general understanding to make the most of your career.

Two excellent dates (and the days in between) for making your mark professionally are the 15th and the 20th of July. This is a time when the Sun moves up high in your horoscope, bringing with it a powerful ego, a sense of responsibility that has an impact on others, and the chance to be recognised. Your positive thinking and deliberate actions will bring you accolades and the opportunity for a new position.

The 23rd of August, the 15th of September and the 4th of October are dates when your confidence and quiet assertiveness will put you ahead of your competitors. You need to execute your plans at these times, but don't cut corners when it comes to problem solving. Physical strength and determination are not enough.

Your communications are highlighted from the 17th to the 20th of November, a time when, at the close of the year, you can once again assert yourself in your professional field.

Career Moves and Promotions

You would do well this year to achieve a better position within the company you currently work for, or elsewhere. Make yourself more aware of your competitors, the marketplace, and what is happening in your industry. As you well know, with economic circumstances tightening around the globe, you need to be a step ahead of your competitors.

When Mercury enters your sixth zone of work around the 3rd of March, you will be busy thinking about how to improve your skills and health so you can produce more in less time. Of course, you will be more efficient, and this is a time when your efforts will be recognised.

INTERVIEW TIMES

If you are going for job interviews, some of the dates that will give you the edge are: the 5th of March, the 9th of May, the 3rd of June, the 25th of June and the 30th of August. Mark these dates in your diary because they are likely to be positive times when interviewers will be pleased with your responses and may develop a liking for you.

With Mercury entering your eleventh house of friendships on the 1st of September, you may have a chance to be introduced, through a mutual friend, to someone in a position of authority. Don't be shy in coming forward if you know there is an opportunity on offer.

Some other dates to look out for are the 7th of September, the 5th of October, the 27th of October, the 22nd of November, and the 15th and 16th of December. Good luck for your search for an improved workplace situation, Scorpio.

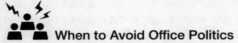

When to Avoid Office Politics

Office politics seem to be part and parcel of work these days, so it's good to know when antagonistic, stressful days are going to ruffle your feathers.

There is nothing worse than feeling stressed out or being made anxious by competitors who would undermine you or spread malicious gossip. At least, through astrology, you can gain an understanding of when your key political dates are going to occur throughout the year.

You're vulnerable around the 20th of January, when the Sun and Saturn are in a conflicting position. Up until at least the middle of the year, Saturn transits in your twelfth house of secrets and hidden enemies. Try to keep your sensitive information close to your chest, and don't share it with anyone, otherwise it could be used against you.

The third week of March, particularly around the 20th and the 21st, could cause some problems as the Sun moves through your zone of workplace activities, openly bringing forth an enemy who is trying to make life difficult for you. Part of the problem may lie in the fact that your contractual arrangement has not been clear enough, which is shown by Saturn creating a difficult aspect to your zone of legalities, morals and spirituality.

Arguments are likely around the 8th of June, when the Sun and Mars create conflict for you. This may spill over into your personal relationships as well. It is best to bite your tongue.

Once again, around the 23rd of September, the Sun moves through the quiet zone of your horoscope, indicating that someone—and this may even be your employer—could try to undermine your integrity and accuse you of doing things of which you are not guilty. However, the more you argue, the guiltier you will seem, so remember that silence is golden.

Disputes over money may be a problem after the 7th of October. You could be short-changed by the paymaster, and this may become a newsworthy item in your office. Try hard this year to maintain a low profile at work, and not divulge too many of your secrets. These seem to be the keys to positive workplace relations for you in 2012.

HEALTH, BEAUTY AND ⊚ LIFESTYLE ⊚

 Venus Calendar for Beauty

Scorpio has Venus taking on an even more important role in love, beauty and affairs of the heart, because it also governs your zone of marriage. Throughout 2012, its movement through different parts of the zodiac will accentuate your beauty and magnetic appeal, and I must say, it is strong even at the most ordinary of times.

But in the mid part of January, around the 14th, to be precise, Venus enters your fifth zone of love affairs and brings with it lovely rays of beauty and power to your Sun sign. You will feel this energy, and will be more likely to connect with others, showing them just who you are and why you are a worthwhile person.

LOVE HIGHLIGHTS

Friendship, love and pleasure are attracted to you after the 2nd of February, and once again around the 5th of March. These dates highlight the pure influence of beauty and elegance upon you as Venus transits key parts of your horoscope.

Along with the movement of Venus, the accent on your Sun sign from one of your ruling planets, Mars, causes you to express yourself in a more forceful way. Even if others haven't quite yet noticed your beauty, you will be making it clear that you are a very worthwhile item.

In September, Venus moves through the highest point in your horoscope, indicating a greater attractiveness all round. You will appeal to others, particularly through your professional activities. After this, your love life will be smooth sailing generally because of your attractiveness. Your social as well as your romantic activities will also be bolstered significantly by this transit.

Showing off Your Scorpio Traits

Each zodiac sign has its own unique power based on the elements and planets that rule it. Unfortunately, most people don't know how to tap into this power and bring out their greatest potential to achieve success in life.

In 2012, it is important for you to reduce tension in your home life. You can't let anything interfere with the quality of the energy that is Scorpio. The transit of Venus in your zone of family affairs and children throughout January and February highlights the fact that dedicating some time early in the year to these areas will reduce the stress levels so you can focus clearly on those other parts of life that give Scorpio such a thrill.

FRIENDSHIP FOCUS

Because your ruling planet, Mars, is spending such a great deal of time in your zone of friendships and life fulfilment in 2012, you will also need to connect more strongly with friends and those whom you may have discarded for some time.

The periods of 2009, 2010 and 2011 were very powerful ones for most Scorpios, and if you are a typical Scorpio, you have been putting considerable energy into work, making money, and becoming financially and professionally secure. Now it's time to turn that around, and give some energy back to others.

After July, you'll find that it's a low-key period—and possibly even a frustrating one—due to the combined influence of Mars and Saturn in the hidden zone of your horoscope. It is important through the months of August and September to eliminate personal frustrations and bad habits that are holding you back.

One of those bad habits is impatience, particularly with trifling matters. Contain your energy and don't fly off the handle over little things. By doing this throughout the last months of the year, you will find yourself developing inner strength and determination and becoming much more focused on what's important and what's not.

Best Ways to Celebrate

Although mentioned in your star sign summary, friendship throughout 2012 is a key ingredient for making yourself happy and, to a large extent, crucial to the way you celebrate life.

If you wish to celebrate this year, why not do so in a less busy arena? With Mars, your ruling planet, in Virgo, there is a hint of modesty and low-key celebration indicated for you. This doesn't mean you don't necessarily have fun, it just shows that your tastes are changing, and that it's quite okay to do things in a not-so-loud and boisterous manner.

Usually, your birthday is one of the most celebratory times of the year. And throughout October and November, depending on the time you were born, we see that Mercury, the planet of humour and laughter, transits your Sun sign. This is just as well, because nearby, Saturn, the sombre and sometimes overly inhibitive planet, needs to take on a bit of light-hearted humour from Mercury.

So celebrate this year by doing something fun, like checking out some comedy while mixing with younger people who are naturally light-hearted and happy. This will rub off on you and give you a feel for what it's like to have a belly laugh and not worry about what anyone else is thinking.

The next most important event would have to be Christmas, and this time, throughout December of 2012, the planets are really focused on the sign of Scorpio, your Sun sign.

At the beginning of December, Saturn, Venus and Mercury, along with one of your karmic planets, indicate that the celebration and joy of life should be found from within, not through anyone else or any particular environment. This is more or less an acknowledgement of yourself, and a deeper acceptance of your good qualities as well as your ability to share them with others in a joyous manner.

KARMA, SPIRITUALITY AND EMOTIONAL ◎ BALANCE ◎

Your spiritual planets are the Moon, Jupiter and Neptune. In 2012, the Moon is in close proximity to progressive Uranus, showing that your service to others through your good work will be one of the key factors in opening up your heart to a greater spiritual dimension. I meant to say that if, previously, you have been attentive to the results of your work, and to the money or power that you achieve through these activities, then this year will be all about forgetting them and instead lifting your game to a point where the quality of the work, and the satisfaction others gain from your input, will be your key focuses.

The Moon has to do with your past karma, so some of your activities will now come to fruition in the area of your work and co-workers.

LUCKY JUPITER

Your future karma planets are Jupiter and Neptune. Jupiter brings with it great opportunities in any sort of partnership this year. That includes business partnerships and personal connections.

In fact, for those of you who are not married, Jupiter is in its finest placement for twelve years. You should avail yourself of the opportunity to unite with someone completely, even if, previously, you have been scared of commitment. You are likely to meet someone beautiful who will satisfy your needs emotionally, physically and spiritually.

Neptune, the slow-moving spiritual planet, continues to transit through your zone of family and home affairs until the end of February and early March. You need to ramp up your activites in that arena to feel spiritually fulfilled this year. If you are able to clarify any of the confusion that remains, when Neptune moves to your zone of love affairs, creativity and children, you'll be in a much, much better position to clearly see what you want from life, and to express your spiritual gifts to the world around you.

2012
MONTHLY & DAILY PREDICTIONS

A MAN BEGINS CUTTING HIS
WISDOM TEETH THE FIRST TIME
HE BITES OFF MORE THAN HE CAN
CHEW.

Herb Caen

◎ JANUARY ◎

 Monthly Highlight

The transits of Venus in your zone of domestics and Jupiter in your intimate area of relationships point to this month being coloured by feelings of warmth and family interactions. You could draw closer to your parents, and may even receive some sort of unexpected inheritance or gift.

After the 13th, Mercury allows you to sign contracts, or at least agree to a new course of action.

The transit of Venus in your zone of love affairs after the 30th foretells not only of your romantic interests and good luck in that area, but also of your creative abilities.

1
Sun

Business matters currently seem to be under a fortunate star for you. You can expect to make some real progress materially, socially and intellectually at the moment.

2
Mon

You'll come to a decision about a business issue or some family friction today. It's imperative that there's no dredging up of old stories. Leave them in the past.

Tues 3
An occasional disapproving word from someone is nothing to be too disheartened about. If this person insists on snapping at you repeatedly, however, then it's high time to speak up.

Wed 4
Don't deny spontaneity in your personality today. You might be absorbed in doing the job right, and are forgetting the greater power of who you *are*. Remain aware.

Thur 5
Recent confusion in your relationships today gives way to an enlightened view of things. Your perspective on a current association may have been skewed as a result of your rose-coloured glasses.

Fri 6
You can either get caught up in the same old rigmarole with family members or present a different approach. A bit of reverse-psychology goes a long way!

Sat 7
It's almost certain you'll take on board a position that will increase your weekly income and add prestige to your daily life.

Sun 8
You'll be tempted to dive into a business deal or residential offer that could put you behind the eight ball financially if you don't read the small print.

9
Mon

After all this time, you still find the same feelings come up in association with a certain situation. It's time you reassessed where you're going with this.

10
Tue

You may become reclusive, shunning contact with others for a while. Your new values will be an orderly existence along with neatness and organisation.

11
Wed

Take some time out to listen to conventional wisdom today, as you may be reckless and fiery. Practical advice may help you channel your energy into productive pursuits.

12
Th

There are prospects for an exciting and nicely challenging day today, but only if you make an effort to clean up that backlog of work!

13
Fri

Don't get carried away with bits and pieces that have no connection to the big picture. Delegate the small stuff so your single focus is on the wider view!

14
Sat

If you're home or job hunting, today is the day when you could find success in the form of an offer or referral. Settle for no less than what you believe is fair!

15
Sun

Take advantage of the great influences coming your way over the next 24 hours. Unhappy family situations reach a turning point and you're the meat in the sandwich.

16
Mon

You won't be satisfied until you have the biggest and best today—everything will be done in a big way.

17
Tues

At the moment, you can channel your moods and energy to provide useful suggestions to loved ones. Do this subtly and you will gain some benefits in a roundabout way.

18
Wed

Sometimes you have to boil down the sap to get to the syrup. Look a little more deeply to see the true worth of a person you met recently. Don't take things at face value for the time being. Wait.

19
Thur

The planets are influencing the forces shaping your professional destiny at the moment. Luckily, your grievance and doubt over a work matter is short lived.

20
Fri

You may feel as though you're being ignored by the people closest to you, but you probably haven't noticed that they have issues, too. Try to be more compassionate just now.

21 *Sat*
You may invite trouble today in your family circle by not agreeing with a 'good' idea. You're bored with tradition, so do your own thing and avoid the hassle.

21 *Sun*
Today, you may not be open in your dealings with others as a means to avoid big, bad egos. You may even be passive-aggressive. Even so, someone will try to bait you.

22 *Mon*
You're more action-oriented today, and want to be the centre of activity. Because of the extravagances, however, this period may burden you with excessive debt.

23 *Tues*
You will go out of your way to impress others with your influence or wealth in an attempt to appear important. Meanwhile, others may be thinking: 'All that glitters is not gold.'

24 *Wed*
Matters of cleanliness and sterile environments are important to you today. You're trying to rediscover parts of yourself that are hidden, and this is the right time for it.

25 *Thur*
You may use your abilities to uncover corruption, or find greater compassion for people who have been victims of the abuses of the world or in your workplace.

26
Fri

Your thinking may be messed up and uncertain. Nervous exhaustion can occur. If you enjoy writing, you can find inspiration in it at this time, and it will even clear your mind.

27
Sat

You stand a very good chance of being used, deceived or taken advantage of in some way today. This is a wonderful time to figure out who your true friends and admirers are.

28
Sun

According to some people, you're not to blame, so stop beating yourself up about it! Your inner self tells you they made their choice, just as you made yours, so rise above the idea of victimhood.

29
Mon

Refrain from talking at people during any meetings today. You want things to work out as you've imagined, so do your best to say things with a smile on your face.

30
Tues

It's an excellent day to make changes to your routine. Find out what's necessary for your long-term goals—these plans are going to be your future foundations!

31
Wed

It's pointless making out that you understand what is going on when those who love you know you have little idea! Embrace the new and be gentle on yourself.

☙ FEBRUARY ☙

Monthly Highlight

Mercury causes confusion and miscommunication with employers. Try to be clearer in describing what you want this month.

A new partnership, possibly of a business nature, may come to pass after the 11th. Don't take too much for granted and move with slow but sure steps.

Mars in your career zone makes you industrious but also very, very competitive. After the 20th, your work and social lives will be closely intertwined.

Thur 1

Discussions about work are high on your agenda at present, but you may be over-reacting to the responses of others to your suggestions. It's early days yet, so don't take no to mean no.

Fri 2

Family members disapprove of what you're doing in your work or your social life. This could create problems for you, but draw a line in the sand and live life on your own terms.

---

3 *Sat*

You are likely to be angry today, and the Moon and Mars combination makes you trigger happy. You need to employ diplomatic means to resolve problems.

4 *Sun / Sat*

'Who rules the roost?' will be an important question in your social affairs today. Ego or power plays make it uncomfortable being in your usual social circle.

5 *Mon / Sun*

Surround yourself with people who've experienced similar things to you. You can gain an all-round understanding, provided you're prepared to accept your faults.

6 *Tues / Mon*

You may be afraid of pooling your resources and physical energies with someone, because you may not be gaining the recognition you desire. Today is a day of spiritual trust.

7 *Wed / Tue*

Today's a full Moon and you'll achieve a great deal, but not if you're engaging other people on your tasks. They could hinder you rather than help.

8 *Thur / Wed*

There's an upswing in your romantic desires, and the Moon and Mars in combination make you impulsive and quite sexual. It could be a fun day.

9
You continue to be playful, and want to explore what's on offer in your personal relationships. You may need to break some boundaries just now.

10
If you're in a business relationship, you may have to decide whether your partner has the same goals as you do, otherwise you could get distracted and start to wonder if the grass is greener on the other side.

11
You're changing your patterns of thinking regarding money, and this is a good thing just now. Curtailing extraneous expenditure will help you save money.

12
If ex-lovers are trying to make a comeback, this could throw you off-kilter today. Think carefully about re-engaging with people who previously did the dirty on you.

13
A chance meeting with an old friend is likely around this time. However, you may realise that you're completely different people now. My, how things change!

14
Unresolved issues with a relative or friend may cause you to travel and inconvenience yourself today. It's probably better to deal with this issue via the telephone.

15

Bury the hatchet now if there are problems on the home front. It's time to move on and remove those negative feelings.

16

Hanging on to the residence you live in is part of an emotional hang-up. Make a clean break, and enjoy some new and exciting exploits in life. Don't fear making a change just now.

17

Love and relationships are playing on your mind. You're wondering whether to force someone's hand in a situation where you're not sure what they want. There's no harm in giving it a little more of a push though, is there?

18

If you're hurt and confused by a certain relationship, it's important to remind yourself that time heals all wounds. Trust in this healing process.

19

There's some confusion about issues in your workplace due to the presence of Neptune. You need to be creative and imaginative in the way you deal with obstructive individuals.

20

It's time to step up your exercise regime. You're probably feeling sedentary at the moment, and need to move that blood of yours around. Get out and about and clear your head.

21 The new Moon means both the Sun and the Moon now occupy your relationship sphere. It's time to clear up any misunderstandings or, better still, start a new relationship. This is an excellent omen for satisfaction.

Tues
Wed

22 A change is as good as a holiday. If you're not getting satisfaction from your existing clientele or friendships, venture forth and seek out new people.

Wed
Thur

23 If your partner has a personal problem, make sure you have time to listen to their grievances. Today's theme is unconditional love, which means you may have to put your own stuff on hold.

Thur

24 You need to empower others as well as yourself today. By helping those around you, they will, in turn, help you. You need to see the bigger picture in your relationships, as well as in your professional life.

Fri
Sat

25 If some of your closest friends don't seem to be open and honest with you, try some different strategies for raising their standards of integrity. Here's a suggestion: straightforwardness.

Sun
Sat

26

~~Mon~~

Sun

Handle the details of a financial transaction yourself rather than trusting them to someone else. If there is any mistrust hanging around just now, you need to do things for yourself.

27

~~Tues~~

Mon

If you take other people's statements too personally, you're doomed to upset your relationships. Don't assume people are levelling their remarks only at you today.

28

~~Wed~~

Tues

Higher education activities will be part of your current cycle. Expanding your knowledge and learning more about different things will interest you.

29

~~Thur~~

Wed

The month finishes on a professional note. You feel as though you have some good luck, but you shouldn't let that deter you from continuing to apply your best efforts.

◉ MARCH ◎

 Monthly Highlight

Venus brings you a mixed bag of social opportunities, but also disagreements this month. You'll be popular with others and your social agenda gets busier after the 9th.

You feel a little inadequate and lacking in self-confidence after the 20th. You may need to brush up your skills before entering a super professional situation.

From the 30th, your ambitions will be intensified, and it's best not to be overly confident.

Fri 1

It's quite alright to be indecisive, as long as you're not going to procrastinate too long. A decision relating to work may bother you today.

---

2 Sat

Show off your best talents to friends without fear of reprise. Don't be scared that you may outshine someone today. It's all about being recognised.

3
Sun

You can dance on the romantic stage of life and attract many new friends just now. There may be the possibility of developing a friendship into a more serious affair.

4
Mon

There's a strong cultural vibe around you just now and you may take an interest in foreign issues, cuisine and people who don't come from where you do.

5
Tues

If you're hiding your talents, it will be pretty hard for you to veil them at the moment. You may need to spend a little time honing your skills and your abilities, but a little discipline will be worth it in the long run.

6
Wed

Don't let fear cripple you. If you have worries about your health or that of someone else, the quickest way to solve this is to get an expert opinion. It's probably nothing.

7
Thur

Your energy is on the increase. However, you may feel self-conscious about doing something right now because of the opinions of others. Do what makes you feel good.

8
Fri

Reassess the work that you do against who you are and what your true talents are. You may be trying to slot into a type of work that's not exactly the best choice.

9

Sat

Mars will provoke you and your partners, both personal and professional, into thrashing out the details of finances. Your value system may be at odds with someone else's.

10

Sun

You could be treading on eggshells to keep the peace at the moment, especially if you're married. Harmony, of course, is essential, but not at the expense of your self-esteem.

11

Mon

Deliberate carefully before passing judgement on a certain issue. A serious conversation will go better if you have your facts to hand.

12

Tues

You could be investing more time than necessary on the tasks that are expected of you. Jupiter makes it easy to get your schedule in order, so why not use these energies wisely? Break things down into their constituent parts, and prioritise.

13

Wed

Home is where the heart is. If you aren't in the place you'd like to be, try enjoying what you have, and stop focusing on what you don't!

14

Thur

Venus is prodding you to travel right now, so it's not a bad idea to get away and explore the hidden side of your personality—and that of your closest mate.

15
Fri
You can't ignore your physical desire just now, with Mercury hinting at the fact that you'll be interested in developing your physical as well as emotional needs. There's a playful energy associated with this planet.

16
Sat
It's all about entertainment just now, so if you've been burning the candle at both ends with work, work and more work, it's time to let your hair down and relax.

17
Sun
Which romantic cherry should you pick from the tree of love? This is the question for some star signs at the moment. There's a challenge in knowing how to sort the men from the boys, so to speak.

18
Mon
Hardworking Saturn doesn't mean that it should all be hard work. A clever approach means that working smart can also yield good results—probably more so than the hard-work angle.

19
Tues
You have an endless supply of energy for projects just now, but your health could suffer. Moderate your timetable so that you can enjoy other things in life as well.

20 **Wed** You're presently confused about your partner— probably their health or their financial situation. But with the Sun influencing them at the moment, you're probably over-reacting.

21 **Thur** You can strike an opportune deal with a high-powered individual today. This person can open a few doors for you, making your work that much more worthwhile.

22 **Fri** You'll be one of the quickest sprinters off the block today, trying to analyse yourself and others. Some of your assessments will be correct, and you'll be in a better position to deal with your relationships as a result.

23 **Sat** A slower, steadier approach seems to be the key today. Others may be hurrying you or trying to reach their objectives more quickly. However, slow and efficient work will win out in the end.

24 **Sun** You could be concerned today if your employer hands you a new set of instructions— complete with fine print. Mistrust could cloud your judgement. Take this as being all in a day's work.

25
Mon

Mental discipline—and a greater degree of concentration on what you're doing—may be difficult just now, but they are important for maintaining your professionalism. Don't allow others to distract you.

26
Tues

You will continue to rush around madly, and possibly not finish the tasks you're supposed to do. You're partly to blame for this, but there are other factors involved, too. At least take responsibility for your part.

27
Wed

You could be lucky just now, but be careful not to lunge at an opportunity. A relaxed and poised attitude will make a greater impression on others.

28
Thur

You may need to take control of a situation if management is out to lunch. This may be a daunting task, but it will reveal some of your hidden talents.

29
Fri

Your progressive methods may be out of step with your peers. It's best not to talk about what you're doing but rather to let the results speak for themselves.

30
Sat

Define your relationships clearly just now, especially those of a social nature. You needn't take heat from those pressuring you to be different. Be true to yourself.

31

Sun

A team effort is what's needed if you're working collaboratively on some ideas. Being an island unto yourself will only serve to alienate you from your friends and their help.

☞ APRIL ☞

 Monthly Highlight

Humility underpins your success this month. After the 23rd, you will have a variety of encounters with people. You'll be tested psychologically, and will certainly gain some new experiences. Don't challenge others.

Health issues after the 29th could bolt you to the ground. It's quite likely that these are more psychological than physical.

Mon 1
You could feel somewhat alone today in looking at your future. Even if you're married or in a committed relationship, you may feel as though you're treading the path alone. Sometimes that's necessary to achieve success, after which you can share the spoils.

2 Tues
You're probably your own worst enemy today, because you're looking at the situation from the wrong perspective. Put a positive spin on wherever it is that you are just now.

3 Wed Don't leave anything to chance today. Manage your personal affairs as efficiently as possible. Remain beyond reproach.

4 Thur Clarity is necessary in your relationships at the moment because Mercury is retrograde. Gain more information about your partner or friend so that you can make a correct assessment. Don't jump to conclusions.

5 Fri Today, you need to manage your time as effectively as possible. Financial matters could drain you of a lot of creative energy. The sooner you get this job out of the way, though, the better.

6 Sat The full Moon today accentuates your focus on money, material goods and finance. An issue relating to your income could finally become clear.

7 Sun Communication with your work colleagues requires you to set your goals together. Find the common thread, and your power as a unit will be greatly enhanced.

8 Mon A stroke of luck could land you a better job, or at least a better position within your organisation during this period. Effectively improving your communication is at the heart of this.

9 Tue Friends are accommodating you just now, and could be willing to visit you rather than vice versa. It's nice to see others making an effort, isn't it?

10 Wed Venus gives you extraordinary charm and luck. Just don't blow it by paying too much attention to the social aspects rather than your business responsibilities.

11 Thur Take a risk today, and ask for what you want. The chances are you'll shock your employer into giving you what you're worth.

12 Fri You have a competitive spirit at the moment, but you must remember to be a good sport as well. You're not always going to win, but it's the development of your skills and the fun you have that counts.

13 Sat You can feel reasonably happy in the role you're playing professionally, but you may need to spend some money to improve your skills.

14 Sun Your expenses could spiral out of control because of a false sense of security. Don't be scared to create a budget for yourself.

15
Mon
Continue to plan your savings and monitor your spending just now. Have a plan for your future security. Something may be amiss in your superannuation arrangement.

16
Tues
You feel idealistic about your relationships today, but could be let down when you don't get as much as you give. Why not try a new strategy?

17
Wed
A superb opportunity for love comes your way as the Moon moves to one of the most prominent romantic parts of your horoscope. You should avail yourself of a new connection just now.

18
Thur
Your reputation will be strongly tied to your love and sexuality at the moment. Maintaining your integrity is all important because this cycle pushes you to try new things.

19
Fri
If you have been looking for a new job, it could be extremely tempting to leave where you are. But you need to realise that this is only a momentary impulse.

20
Sat
The Sun moves to your zone of marriage and partnerships. It creates a mixed bag for you just now, with love and hate featuring equally in your mind. Try to emphasise the love side of things, though.

21 **Sun**

You're in the slipstream of cultural and artistic happenings today. You need to open yourself up to the possibility of trying things differently. An invitation to an unusual gathering will be most interesting.

22 **Mon**

You need a coherent synthesis to bring your relationships together and push them to a new level. Things will be much smoother and happier as a result.

23 **Tues**

Try not to rely too much on pharmaceuticals to solve your health problems at the moment. There are alternatives, and you may need to investigate theses today.

24 **Wed**

You may be dealing with a 'terrorist' on the work front. Try to maintain your calm, and don't retaliate.

25 **Thur**

If you are invited to a function, you need to consider dressing more elegantly. Sure, comfort is great, but the circumstances may demand a little sacrifice.

26 **Fri**

You need plenty of sunlight just now, especially if you find yourself in a situation indoors where everyone is quivering over nothing. Get out and enjoy the fresh air.

27
Sat-

Theoretical ideas are fine, but their practical application is the only way to test them. Be courageous in implementing your concepts just now.

28
Sun-

You are required to lead others, but may be fearful of ridicule. You must overcome these apprehensions.

29
Mon

Your work now requires neutral service. Your arch rival may be causing you difficulties, but serving them for the moment will ultimately be in your best interest.

30
Tues

If you need to make a refusal today, do so, but you needn't do it in a rude fashion. This will work against your best interests in the end.

☉ MAY ☉

Monthly Highlight

This month, much of your activity will centre around shared resources, taxes and other savings. These effects will be more pronounced after the 22nd, but it's best to be prepared prior to then.

There's even greater focus on your career after the 31st, when Mercury casts its favourable glance on your work sphere. Clarify your plans before moving into gear.

Wed 1
You're making mountains out of mole hills by multiplying the problem. The trick is to reduce your tasks to ridiculously small components.

Thur 2
Relationships may intensify because you feel like you are fooling around rather than getting serious. This may cause you to step away for a while and recollect your energies.

Fri 3
If you are unmarried and looking for security, the danger is that you may settle for second best. Stick to your guns, and raise your standards.

4
Sat

You may be invited to make a donation, but if it's not coming from the heart the results will not be good, particularly on a karmic level. Say no if you don't have the money.

5
Sun

Occasionally, a wake-up call is necessary to spare us from disastrous friendships and relationships. Heed the advice of a close friend just now.

6
Mon

Stop relying on the approval of others to make your decisions today. Trust your discretion, and the conclusions you draw will be correct.

7
Tues

You feel lazy today, and this is because you have been overheated by work and the demands of family. You have full permission to a be couch potato.

8
Wed

There is some disruption about you, but at the end of the day this will give you a chance to try something different by stepping away from the usual routine. Enjoy this distraction.

9
Thur

You are concerned that lust rather than love may be dominating one of your relationships at the moment. The prospects seem hollow, so refuse yourself the half or quarter of a relationship.

10
Fri

You could feel awkward if you need to exhibit bias towards one person or another in your workplace. It is only natural to express preferences, so don't feel guilty.

11
Sat

You may be concluding some learning or study that will allow you to bend the rules and achieve something new in your life. Keep bending. There is no progress without deviation.

12
Sun

You may have a rough-and-ready lunch prepared that is not altogether appetising, but the company will be great. I guess it is better than cordon bleu cuisine with boring friends.

13
Mon

Any sort of feeble experiment with love just now will destroy your chances of making the relationship solid and secure. Don't do it if you are not serious.

14
Tues

Some Scorpios may be recovering from a separation, and it will take time and intelligence to deal with such a transition. Keep working at it, and eventually things will pan out to your liking.

15
Wed

Strong demands may be placed on you, and it will be imperative to hold your head high and accept what is thrown at you just now. You may not feel good about it, but you will get additional respect.

16
Thur

Feeling sad and expressing this to others only limits your ability to connect with them and increase your opportunity for popularity. You need to re-route your attitude into a more positive lane.

17
Fri

You may simply be arguing with someone to strike a pose or stroke your own ego, when doing this will not get you what you want. Give the other person a chance to put forward their views.

18
Sat

If someone is obstructing you just now, your desire to race to the finish line will create tension and frustration. You must be unambiguous in your demands.

19
Sun

Your sense of humour may well be appreciated by people your own age, but if you happen to be in the company of anyone a little more stodgy and old-fashioned than your usual acquaintances today, you might raise a few eyebrows.

20
Mon

There is no need to suffer fools gladly just now. Someone has become nastier and nastier, and you know they are a bad seed. Cut them out of your life and get back on the road to happiness.

21

If, today, you feel incompetent and that time is crawling at a snail's pace, it means you either have to try something new or approach your work in a more productive manner.

22
Wed

You may be threatened in a subtle way by an older character who only means well. Set aside your sensitivities and take what they say on board. It will be timely advice.

23
Thur

One good deed deserves another. Repaying a favour may be hanging over your head, but you don't have the time to square this debt off immediately.

24
Fri

You may be wary of dealing with children or younger people, but your understanding may be clarified now by a new discovery. This should greatly improve your relationship.

25
Sat

If you can also introduce aesthetics and creative flair into your work, you'll add a new dimension to your function. Consider the ways in which you can embellish your craft.

26
Sun

Your mailbox needs to be of epic proportions to handle the deluge of information heading your way. If you've got too much mail, you are not handling the junk filters properly. Consider these.

27
Mon
Even if you amend your manners, personality and ways, you'll find that things remain relatively unchanged at the moment. There is nothing much more you can do about it.

28
Tues
Stock-standard morons abound in the world, so you are certain to bump into the odd one from time to time. Today could be one of those times.

29
Wed
You may be tentative about driving somewhere, especially if you've never been there before. Come on, Scorpio, incite the spirit of adventure.

30
Thur
Someone may obstruct you, possibly a friend, because they are numb to your ongoing principles. How many times do you have to tell them? Never again.

31
Fri
You may be taking on the responsibilities of other family members only to find that they never learn to grow up and do things for themselves. You can't be landed with these obligations anymore. Dispense with their victimhood.

◎ JUNE ◎

 Monthly Highlight

You may meet someone who has a significant impact on your life after the 5th. Venus may even tug at your heartstrings, giving you a sense of romantic connectedness with someone in your workplace. Tread carefully.

Legal matters after the 28th may require some delicate handling. Religion and higher education issues are also on the cards. If you want some time out, this is a good month to arrange for some travel.

Sat 1

You might start to feel guilty today, by pointing out the faults of someone else. But if you are going to improve the overall situation, you must speak up.

Sun 2

Erase some of the work you have done because it seems as though it's been invalidated by someone else. Starting over may seem like a daunting task, but the second round will work out much better.

3
Mon You may wish to travel south, but it should only be for a holiday. The omen is not good if you are contemplating a permanent shift.

4
Tues You need to qualify a person before allowing them to close a deal. If this person is unknown to you, tread warily.

5
Wed You'll be punishing yourself if you spend big on a fashion fad. Don't allow advertising and conditioning to dictate your decisions.

6
Thur You may be somewhat disappointed by a journey today. You may not plan adequately, and feel as though time and money has been wasted.

7
Fri Your mind is thinking about practical matters, but at the same time, your spiritual insights will rise, allowing you to make decisions based on hunches rather than logic. Go with it.

8
Sat A superficial welcome may leave you high and dry today. You may have organised yourself well only to find yourself in the company of shallow individuals.

9
Sun Work pressures don't allow you the opportunity to take time out for your family. This could cause some tensions on the home front, and will require some delicate balancing.

Mon 10 Timing is everything today if you want to deal with bureaucracy in the most efficient manner. Plan to call into work during off-peak periods to cut through the workload and get the job done.

Tues 11 It seems like today could be an ongoing trial for you, in that you must keep your head down and focus on the work at hand. A culprit is wasting your time and you need to read them the riot act.

Wed 12 You could be censored for speaking the truth, and it is up to you how you handle that. Will you say more of the same, or button your lips for the sake of peace?

13 Thur If you want to become successful, you sometimes need to mimic your mentors. However, do this in a way that stamps your own individuality on what you are doing.

14 Fri Good luck comes with responsibility, but today, it's a case of an unpleasant situation due to someone's repeated violation of your space. You'll need to be quietly assertive in how you handle this.

15 Sat What starts out as a sensible function or workplace party could end up a horrid dream for you. Be prepared to leave early.

16
Sun

Accepting a better position with a greater financial remuneration comes with consequences—and that means greater accountability.

17
Mon

You may be surprised to discover a new location that, previously, was completely off your radar. If you are planning to make a move, this could be ideal.

18
Tues

You may need to take some temporary financial measures to bridge one situation to another. You must cast aside your paranoia, however, because you're worrying about nothing.

19
Wed

Your responses today should be kind and courteous. Even if you don't get on well with someone, this could be the action that starts to mend the relationship.

20
Thur

You could regret impromptu gestures of generosity, especially if you're giving away money or things to someone you scarcely know. It's best to appraise the credentials of anyone you meet just now.

21
Fri

If you're revisiting the past, particularly the affairs of your partner, you're creating a rod for your own back. Let go of the past and look to the future.

22
sat

It's best to keep some of your personal matters personal, especially in the workplace today. Someone, perhaps a secretary, may be overhearing what you are saying, and news sure does travel fast, doesn't it?

23
Sun

You have to dedicate much more time to a particular activity if you want to become great at it. Success is not something that accidentally falls in your lap, it requires a lot of hard work, but you realise this.

24
Mon

Performing an audit or some sort of check on your work is necessary but it could fuel some anxiety. If you've done your job properly, you should be relaxed and not have to give this another thought.

25
Tues

A friend may be disregarding the help that's been offered to them, and you are in two minds as to whether or not to say something. If you're a true friend, you'll do it in a polite manner.

26
Wed

You must let your strength shine forth because this will be a source of comfort and inspiration to a friend just now. Your friend's fortunes may be on the wane.

27 Thur
While abbreviating what you say, you can leave yourself open to criticism. Expand on what you mean so there is no room for ambiguity. This way people will understand where you are coming from.

28 Fri
You may need to make alternative plans when an invitation is shut down today. No use crying over spilt milk, as they say. Try something different.

29 Sat
You are ready tackle almost any challenge just now, and this will increase your sense of self-confidence. However, if you need to involve someone else, they may hold you back.

30 Sun
You need to unlock the executive within yourself. By doing so, you can welcome some additional gold, cash and admiration from others.

⊚ JULY ⊚

Monthly Highlight

With Mars entering your twelfth zone of secrets after the 29th, you should take care in the lead-up, with friends and siblings in particular.

Misunderstandings over money could mar your otherwise good relations. Be clear in your desires, and firm if you do not accept what others are demanding.

Mon 1
You have to be rigorous in restricting people's access to you today. You need to simplify your life and maintain a low-key profile to find happiness.

Tues 2
A minor health issue may not be a concern to you. If anything, it will simply irritate, eroding your valuable time.

Wed 3
You can apply creative accounting techniques to the way you earn and save money just now. A friend has some valuable advice.

4
Thur
An unexpected letter will have you scratching your head. Is it good news or not? That's like asking if the cup is half empty, or half full. This bit of information will rely on your perspective.

5
Fri
You will endeavour to put more effort into your work and to clean up your act from this point. A harmless criticism could be the catalyst for this.

6
Sat
You could receive mixed signals from the person you love most. Try to get clarification rather than playing the guessing game.

7
Sun
Your vitality is up now, but you must rest on your laurels for the time being. Continue to improve your diet and make time to exercise.

8
Mon
The Sun in Saturn causes some complications and additional responsibilities over paperwork. You would like to avoid this, but simply can't.

9
Tues
You're optimistic and probably a little too generous with someone just now. Wait to see their reactions before giving them the whole kit and caboodle.

10
Wed
You mustn't lose your temper today. You could be livid about an event over which you have no control. Getting angry will only inflame the situation.

Thur 11 Relatives may be annoying, but you have no choice but to make yourself present out of courtesy. You'll probably wonder how you ended up with this bunch of people as relatives. You can choose your friends, but not family.

Fri 12 It is an inspiring day in which you can gain new ideas to further your own interests and ambitions. Try to think outside the square.

Sat 13 The day can go either way, depending on how you treat people. Although someone may be irritating, there is something to be gained from what they have to say.

Sun 14 You need to curtail your desire make your opinions known for the moment, even though you are probably right. Your quiet actions will speak louder than words.

Mon 15 You may temporarily have to work with someone who has a completely different style to you. Try to learn from each other, and this could enhance your productivity.

Tues 16 An advancement of sorts can be expected just now, but you have to be creative and research-oriented to bring out your best flavours. A secret may be revealed.

17
Wed
If you are looking to attract intriguing people, this could be just the day for that. Someone of unusually high intelligence will inspire you.

18
Thur
You need to be tasteful in your dress and also in your choice of company to be an even bigger hit than you have been. Avoid copying others so you will at least be individualistic.

19
Fri
If you are looking for a tactic to impress the people you work with, you need to improve on your track record to give them reassurance. This should work wonders.

20
Sat
You may be promised something, and its fine, but then someone reneges. An addictive personality, possibly a woman, may be part of the problem.

21
Sun
This is a time when improved relationships are assured. A little retail therapy, keeping in mind your nearest and dearest, will be an effective way to draw them closer.

22
Mon
Changes being made in your domestic sphere, either by you or someone else, will cause you to re-evaluate who you are and where you wish to be emotionally.

23
Tues

Spend some quiet time with friends and family just now. It is an opportunity for you to discuss some economic issues that previously may have been swept under the rug.

24
Wed

You could be obsessing about someone just now, which is scattering your energies. If you have a problem with them, call and talk to them.

25
Thur

You will be rethinking your association with one or more of your current friends. Although they may be fun and desirable to be with, you're questioning the long-term benefits.

26
Fri

You need to offset the rigours of day-to-day living by enlightening yourself with some musical entertainment. Get out and listen to an uninhibited rock band or some classical music, whichever is your preference.

27
Sat

You mustn't duplicate the past, especially if you are feeling disconnected from the person you love. Try to get to know each other a little more, and do so without too many others around. Quiet time is needed.

28
Sun

Pride is not going to help resolve your romantic issues today. If you are outraged at something that has been said or done, don't patronise the other person. Try to be conciliatory.

29
Mon

If an old flame re-enters your life, you must ask yourself an important question: whether or not you have exhausted every aspect of that friendship.

30
Tues

If you are not happy with the medical practitioner you have been using, you can always change to someone new. Investigate the options, and don't be scared to ask questions.

31
Wed

Excuses are not going to wash too well, and direct and honest communication on your part will be the best bet to achieve your objectives today.

⊚ AUGUST ⊚

Monthly Highlight

With the Sun moving into your career zone after the 8th, an exciting new chapter begins for your professional activities. A coveted position may finally be yours.

If you contemplated developing your skills as an artist or in another creative activity, the movement of Venus into your zone of higher learning after the 15th gives you the opportunity to study or travel with people associated with these activities. An increased interest in other cultures also is indicated.

Thur 1   You can adapt if you are permitted to do so. Someone wants you to change and is demanding the impossible, which is not going to happen just now.

Fri 2   You need to change your fiscal policy, especially if your partner or lover is condemning you for your spending habits. But you mustn't do this under pressure.

3
sat

If someone can make you smile, even when you are terribly angry, then you know you have a special connection. If that is the case, you can consider yourself lucky today.

4
sun

Being overly serious with someone is no way to get them to speak about their feelings. Lighten up a little, and they will share much more with you.

5
Mon

Your feelings are misplaced, and you're unable to understand someone's responses today. You may need to talk to a third party, a mutual friend.

6
Tues

If you have a business idea, you need to be careful you are not simply running on instinct. First, do some research and study the trends in that particular industry.

7
Wed

You might need to do something artificially to win the approval of the people with whom you live and work. You need to step outside the normal channels to prove your point.

8
Thur

Don't book accommodation before first checking it. In your excitement, it may be the furthest thing from your mind, but it could present a problem if not properly researched.

Fri 9

There might be an exhilarating sensation of love at first sight today, but this passion may be short lived. Enjoy an amorous adventure.

Sat 10

Although you might want to move or change, you may have to face the stark reality of saving harder for what you want right now.

Sun 11

Visiting friends, especially if it's for superficial reasons, won't be satisfying today. You may need to stay at home and delve a little deeper into yourself to determine what you truly want.

Mon 12

Your love life should evolve, and you should feel blessed by your partner today. Expect lots of tender loving affection.

Tues 13

Be enthusiastic and upbeat about what's happening in your life. Issues of health may be high on your agenda, so you need to be cautious of what you eat. Extra acidity may be an issue.

Wed 14

Difficulties in your work could centre on hidden things that take you by surprise. You need to be patient, and patiently endure the troubles.

15 Thur
Your imagination might give way to ideas in areas you have not considered before. New avenues or a new frame of mind could come in sequential stages. A novel idea for a new source of income is a possibility. Such business plans are exciting.

16 Fri
Even though you are working with a great deal of diligence, you may not be able to sidestep the hostile attitudes of people around you. This is, once again, based on pure jealousy.

17 Sat
You have a renewed appetite for work at the moment, so go for it with all your might. Although Mars and Saturn have been causing troubles, you will get through this, so stick to it.

18 Sun
Avoid any intoxicants just now. You need to be clear-minded and focused on what you are doing. This will help you in both your work and your personal relationships.

19 Mon
You need to avoid topics that are going to create problems for you with friends. Although your conversation will be lively, try to keep it on a topic that is less contentious.

20 Tues
You may want to take some risks at the moment, especially with your work. Mars does create strife, but because of your current luck, it could work out for you.

21
Wed

Remain calm and collected, because so much may be happening today that you become disoriented. If that is the case, your decisions may be off-course.

22
Thur

If you are looking to conquer your social landscape, you need to remove all self-doubts today. Some great opportunities with friendships arise.

23
Fri

Closing off some problematic issues may take longer than expected. It's not the right time to indulge in new business activities, especially if they are speculative.

24
Sat

Your energy levels should soar just now, with Mars entering your Sun sign. Your goals will seem insurmountable, but you could be a little tactless in your interactions.

25
Sun

You can make your dreams come true right now. If you've waited a long time, real opportunities to make your concepts concrete will arise. You have the support of a friend.

26
Mon

You mustn't be authoritarian in the way you deal with people today, even if you *are* in a position of authority. A gentle hand will win you a few extra friends.

27 _Thurs_
You need to clear up problems and misunderstandings, especially if they are of a contractual nature. By looking through the fine print and getting general consensus, your tensions will ease.

28 _Wed_
There are good prospects for your career just now, but you mustn't embellish or exaggerate your abilities. Someone will see straight through you.

29 _Thur_
As fast as you want to finish something today, your system and your brain may be in go-slow mode. Don't rush things—you will do a much better job if you just keep cool.

30 _Fri_
Even taunts and insults won't affect you adversely today, because you feel so good about yourself. Let others' comments slide off you like water off a duck's back.

31 _Sat_
If you stay in a situation in which you are unproductive, it doesn't do anyone any good. Turn off the computer, go to the park or watch a movie—do anything to switch off for a few hours.

⊛ SEPTEMBER ⊛

Monthly Highlight

A transformative effect on your finances occurs this month, and it will be a very long cycle, commencing after the 6th. You must learn to re-evaluate and organise your finances if you are to develop positive strategies for security.

Friendships abound after the 11th, and you'll be in touch with many new people, some of whom you initially thought may not be your cup of tea, but you'll be pleasantly surprised.

It's all systems go in your work after the 21st, with Venus conjoining your career zone. All sorts of personal and business relationships work well under this transit, so you can expect an exciting and productive time.

Sun 1

You can enjoy the games of love today, but you mustn't let that deter you from the responsibilities at hand. A little fun and a little bit of business is the perfect balance.

2 Mon Your family may turn on you just now, because you have revealed too much of your private affairs to them. Keep things closer to your chest.

3 Tues You may have to act as a go-between in solving a dispute between two friends today. Don't shrink back from it.

4 Wed As a result of applying some diplomacy in your workplace, you'll progress quickly in your career. Expect a happy surprise today in your work arena.

5 Thurs This is a great time to achieve a new level of understanding with your partner or loved one. Be a little more patient in your relationships.

6 Fri You'll experience an overwhelming feeling of amorous sensations around this time. If you are in a relationship, you'll know exactly what to do. If not, you could be in for some frustration!

7 Sat You mustn't allow yourself to be drawn in by the promise of easy money. Qualify the credentials of salespeople and smooth talkers.

8 Sun Important changes are taking place within you, and others may not be able to understand what is going on. In friendship, it is worthwhile explaining yourself to create greater understanding.

Mon 9 You could be extremely irritable today, and this has to do with playing the money game. Your sexual life will be bright, however.

10 Tues You have some agreeable meetings just now, but you must still be vigilant because wolves in sheep's clothing may abound. Don't believe everything you hear today.

11 Wed You'll be feeling comfortable about your belief system but someone may try to deter you from your path just now. Remain firm but diplomatic.

12 Thur You could take on too many burdens today, simply for the sake of trying to please everyone. You need to make the call when enough is enough.

13 Fri You could feel a little agitated just now, and there could be a secret that you want to share but know you can't. Simply forget it.

14 Sat Today, you'll succeed in friendship without too much effort. Eliminate those who are of no use to you anymore. Focus on the ones who reciprocate.

15 Sun
Your success in your social life is assured, but meanwhile, you mustn't neglect those who supported you in the past. Make a extra effort with them just now.

16 Mon
You're profitable just now, because the Moon is in your zone of income. Take stock of the situation, and enjoy the extra cash on hand.

17 Tues
Don't involve your friends, even the closest ones in your group, in some of your private problems. Sometimes it is wise to maintain confidentiality.

18 Wed
A neighbour could be causing you some problems today. It's best to send a letter rather than confront them face to face.

19 Thur
Be vigilant in business at present, but also share your successes with those who helped along the way. Don't run the risk of alienating anyone.

20 Fri
You get a green light for a project today, when previously you thought it was dead in the water. An employer is watching you carefully—and quite pleased with what he or she sees right now.

Sat 21 A love affair may hinge on your financial needs, and if this is the basis for it, you can rest assured it will come unstuck. It should be about love for love's sake, nothing more.

Sun 22 Family problems can be solved today, but only if you have roundtable discussions. Don't make other people's decisions for them.

Mon 23 You should maintain satisfactory health, but you won't if you're running here, there and everywhere. Try to create a more workable schedule.

Tues 24 It is a perfect day to resume your studies, and if an exam is on the cards, you should do well.

Wed 25 You can be very charming just now and your family will notice this. Try not to incite jealousy, however. Keep a new relationship under wraps for the time being.

Thurs 26 Look at building up your assets, which you could do by using the equity in your home. Investigate what's on offer, and how much your property is worth.

27
Fri

Try to be more flexible and forgiving of your children if you are a parent. You could be finding communication with them difficult at the moment.

28
Sat

An important change may take place in your most personal relationship today. You and your partner could be out of sync. Rectify it.

29
Sun

If you are not able to control yourself, you may not have an excuse for doing the wrong thing. Containment and impulse control are the key words today.

30
Mon

Someone is playing double agent—being two-faced—and you may realise a little too late. Once you know, however, there will be some changes afoot.

◎ OCTOBER ◎

Monthly Highlight

After the 7th, you'll be much more withdrawn than normal and will probably need a good rest. This needn't be a lonely time, but you should use your withdrawal in a positive and constructive way. In other ways, you can be helping others who are having their own problems, and could be called upon to surrender some time on compassionate grounds.

Between the 9th and the 16th, be careful not to let money get in the way of good relationships. You may find yourself having to defend the way you earn, save and spend money to someone close to you. Cool, clear discussions are in order.

With Venus transiting your zone of social activities after the 19th, you will express yourself well socially, artistically and romantically. This is a feel-good time when warm friendships will reinvigorate your faith in humankind.

The Sun enters your Sun sign after the 24th and this brings with it an upswing and physical vitality.

Tues 1
If you are not in good shape physically, you'll need to take some immediate steps to rectify that. Anyone for the gym?

Wed 2
If you can get through your work quickly today, you'll later have the perfect opportunity to spend some quality time with your loved one. Don't let stormy relations mar the evening.

Thur 3
The stars are shining on you in your relationships, and partnerships in business projects are also favoured just now.

Fri 4
Even if you are in the midst of a conflict over money, try to show the highest degree of diplomacy. Common sense will be your saviour today.

Sat 5
Consolidate your activities, and try to eliminate those things that are chewing up the most time and yielding you the smallest results at the moment.

Sun 6
Pamper yourself a little today, and don't be afraid to spend a bit of money. You will feel so much better for it.

Mon 7 You may realise you are walking into a disagreement, but strangely, you may want to. However, this is not the best course of action this time. Avoidance is the best solution for now.

Tues 8 You can expect some sudden changes or upheavals, which has to do with a decision you made. No one is going to like everything you say or do, so get used to it.

Wed 9 Your professional life could be in danger if you dig in your heels and don't play with the other kids in the playground on their terms. Try to be more flexible just now.

Thur 10 If you're asking for the impossible from your partner, you may find that you get nothing in return. Your spouse's work schedule may be too demanding for your liking at the moment.

Fri 11 Take a little more rest somehow, because workplace commitments could be frazzling your nerves. Put work out of your mind, especially at bedtime.

Sat 12 Don't provoke your partner by superimposing your own feelings on them today. As long as you ask questions, you won't be putting your foot in it.

13 Sun
A group or crowd environment may not be exactly what you had in mind, and this could irritate you. If you aren't comfortable, leave.

14 Mon
A new phase of life is going to take place shortly, but first you need to eliminate any skeletons in the closest, or at least confront them honestly. Once this is done, the new cycle can begin.

15 Tues
Workplace negotiations could be getting bogged down in details. Impatience will bring out the worst side of your nature. Do something else to break the cycle of frustration.

16 Wed
You'll conclude a business deal today, only because you're exhibiting extreme self-confidence. You are inspiring just now.

17 Thurs
Don't avoid the financial odds and ends that need tidying up at present. It may be easier to turn a blind eye, but inwardly, it's bothering you. Get out the calculator, your pen and paper, and systematically work through the issues.

18 Fri
Weight-reduction methods may not be working for you. The secret is not to eat as much as you usually do, and to consider good food combinations.

Sat 19 You may try to buy love or win the affection of someone through gifts. That won't work. It's better to open your mind and be more tolerant.

20 Sun There is some great progress in your work just now, and a contractual glitch may be resolved. The journey will be problematic but productive.

21 Mon You may want a peaceful day, but will have to deal with three or four problems at once. You should be called an extreme juggler just now.

22 Tues Try to create a better-organised timetable, and adhere to it so you won't be so overwhelmed by your obligations. There could be some disturbance due to the unexpected changing of an appointment by a friend.

23 Wed You should add strength of character, ambition and a reflection of your character to your home environment. You need to feel comfortable in your home.

24 Thur A stormy relationship needn't mean the end of it. Try to get a clearer view of your life and what you both want from each other just now.

25 Fri You could be speculative right now, and are not thinking straight. If you need to gamble, gamble half or a quarter of what you first intended to.

26 Sat

Love affairs continue to dominate your mental landscape today. If you are excessively optimistic you could be in for a heavy fall.

27 Sun

You could succeed in your career during this period, but this will only happen by being prudent and showing due diligence and care in everything you do. A tough project may bring out your best talents.

28 Mon

You may have some new and original ideas, but are scared to share them with others. Keep one trustworthy person around to use as a sounding board.

29 Tues

Don't worry if you have a small failure just now. This is the way to learn from your mistakes and grow stronger.

30 Wed

You may find that your sexual energy is waning at the moment, just at a time when your partner is becoming more interested. Compromise is the name of the game.

31 Thur

Today, a problem that has been bothering you may suddenly vanish, as if by magic. Don't question it, just enjoy the rest of the day!

◎ NOVEMBER ◎

 Monthly Highlight

Saturn enters your Sun sign and this begins a two-and-a-half-year cycle, bringing with it some heavy responsibilities, but, at the same time, a chance to accomplish a great deal. You mustn't shrink back from the challenges that are offered to you by life just now.

Friendships will be low-key after the 9th. You may find yourself having to be secretive or could be left in the dark by someone. Issues of taboo surrounding relationships are also indicated, so be careful with the types of friends you choose.

You are quick off the mark, both verbally and physically. Now, too, is the time, with Mercury and Mars positively influencing you, to take up a new exercise regime. These energies will intensify up to and including the 26th, when you might be a little too aggressive for your own good. Tone it down.

Fri 1 You should listen to the advice of your partner when it comes to money matters just now. Otherwise, your pride could be your downfall.

2
Sat

There are certain financial traps you are not aware of just now. You need to be clear in what you hope to achieve. Professional advice should be sought.

3
Sun

You may not feel as though you're being aggressive in your social group today, but someone may call you on this anyway. Avoid quarrelling because they have only the best intentions.

4
Mon

If there is a change in the weather, you need to be prepared for it, because it may adversely affect your health. Don't forget to take some additional warm garments just in case.

5
Tues

Today, it is important to reconnect with your father or some important male authority figure. Some good advice will hold you in good stead.

6
Wed

You're adding extra spending to your budget that could leave you seriously jeopardised in the future. Cut back on bad habits such as alcohol, smoking and sweets. Your health will improve as well.

7
Thur

You may be feeling insecure in your job, and this is because you are comparing yourself to others. Stop.

Fri 8
You could be caught off guard by someone's flattery just now. Read between the lines because they have an ulterior motive.

9 Sat
You could be tired of socialising, and one-night stands if you are single. This could commence a period of romantic stability.

10 Sun
You're offered a chance to enjoy a fun night out, but would prefer to spend it alone. Trust your instincts—you don't have to go out every night.

11 Mon
Recovering a lot of lost energy is necessary now. A couple of days of self-containment will make a world of difference to you.

12 Tues
You mind is very settled and you're clearer in your purpose at present. Share some of your noble and uplifting ideas with someone interested in your wellbeing.

13 Wed
You are at the top of your game now, and your motivation is high. You may, however, outshine someone, and this could upset them. Be more sensitive.

14 Thur
You have to be authoritarian and a little ruthless when it comes to money today. Although your family may not like your decision, it is in their best interests.

15 Fri

A radical change will be applied to your earning and spending habits just now. Saving, of course, depends not on what you earn, but how little you spend. That's the secret.

16 Sat

You'll continue to curb your appetite, and may even travel somewhere to listen to a lecture or get more information on improved health techniques today.

17 Sun

Don't blindly believe everything someone says—for example, on the Internet. Do your own independent research.

18 Mon

You could find yourself further and further away from your objectives today, getting waylaid by superfluous interests. Finetune your activities to achieve your desired goal.

19 Tues

You may wish to conduct business at home for a while. If it is possible, you will be better able to manage your work and family affairs.

20 Wed

Your mental faculties are finely tuned, and you will be applying them to understanding your history and mistakes more clearly. It's a psychological sort of day.

21 Thur Your lover may be tactless today, and you could retaliate as a result. Relationships with your co-workers might also require a lighter touch.

22 Fri You may be sentimental, even teary today, and you need to explain why to someone—otherwise they might react too harshly. Time alone, for a little while at least, is a good idea.

23 Sat An otherwise pleasant cup of coffee could turn stormy with the evocation of some strong words today. Measure what you say before saying it.

24 Sun Doing your best simply to please someone else is an incorrect approach. You should do your best to do your best and, if others like it, great.

25 Mon Being uptight for a protracted period of time is only going to affect you physically. Learn the art of relaxation.

26 Tues You'll be extremely efficient today, but efficiency has no place in the bedroom! Relax and enjoy yourself.

27 Wed You need to stick to your guns, even if others are trying to distract you from what you are doing. Don't doubt your decisions today.

28
Thur

A short journey could bring you a wealth of information just now. Take care not to spend too much money though. Savings are on your mind.

29
Fri

Spiritual transformation could be an idea you touch upon at some point today. Discussions about metaphysical topics also interest you.

30
Sat

Your sexual appetite may be momentarily out of sync with your partner's. Fortunately, this is a passing phase, so don't worry about it too much.

⊚ DECEMBER ⊚

Monthly Highlight

You're clever with money, so why not devise a new system to increase your cash flow after the 12th? Toss around some ideas with a friend.

Travels are indicated after the 28th, which is perfect and in keeping with your Christmas festivities.

Sun 1
You may revisit your past, or else someone from your past may make contact with you just now. This should be fun, but it may not be a relationship that will continue.

Mon 2
Get out the travel brochures—because Christmas is just around the corner, you have itchy feet, and now is the time to get away.

Tues 3
You could feel depressed that you haven't achieved all the goals you set out to this year. But don't despair. Collect yourself and re-establish your schedule.

---

4 Wed
You could be looking at another promotion or some form of distinction that gives you a sense of pride. Continue to control your budget, however.

5 Thur
What starts as an affair of the heart could end up in tatters. Get to know someone a little better before committing to them.

6 Fri
Don't lend money to friends. This can cause no end of troubles. Respectfully decline. Be honest with your friends, and tell them no if your conscience doesn't feel right.

7 Sat
There are changes in your peer group just now, and you will need to anchor some of your friends and give them a sense of direction.

8 Sun
It's time for you to decide whether you want something, or you don't. You can't have it both ways.

9 Mon
As a result of taking time out, you will feel refreshed and your health should start getting back to where it used to be. Break the cycle of tension by heading out with a friend.

10 Tues
You're excited by the prospect of new professional changes. Talk to your employer if you are on speaking terms.

11 *Wed* Hard work is one thing, but smart work is another. You need to combine both of them now to achieve the optimum results.

12 *Thur* Perseverance in your working life is essential. Don't give up just yet, even if it seems as though it's taking a long time to get to your goal.

13 *Fri* Be careful not to lose money. Pay strict attention to your valuables today. Something may go missing.

14 *Sat* An unexpected problem with a friend may require you to visit them and put other matters on hold. Your compassion will be appreciated.

15 *Sun* You may have had enough of family troubles and responsibilities. There is no harm in walking away and letting others deal with them, at least for the time being.

16 *Mon* You'll have great satisfaction from a job well done just now. If your sleeping patterns are disturbed, try some herbs to help you rest.

17 *Tues* You may have to hide a love affair from someone in your family, or a friend, as they may not approve. But, at the end of the day, it is no one else's business anyway.

18
Wed

You feel creative and physically active just now. Your competitive urges are strong. As long as you direct them to the right areas you will have no problems.

19
Thur

There could be some issues with your chest or your lungs at the moment. Make sure you get enough air and try to avoid cigarette smoke, whether you are a smoker or not.

20
Fri

You will be working desperately to complete your tasks before Christmas. Don't run yourself ragged. You could always resume them in the new year.

21
Sat

You need to change your location of work, or at least temporarily move to a different office. Someone may be annoying you or hindering your progress at the moment.

22
Sun

Don't let gossip disturb you or throw you off-course. Some malicious rumour could overshadow your best efforts. Ignore cheap talk for now.

23
Mon

You could be intoxicated by the idea of marriage, a long-term commitment or the ideal of love. Get real before you fantasise too much, however.

24 Tues

Taking a trip just now is an excellent idea, but family Christmas commitments may stifle you. Learning a language could be an alternative form of satisfaction.

25 Wed

Merry Christmas, Scorpio! You will be rather withdrawn today, but it doesn't mean you can't have a good time as well.

26 Thur

You could be excessive at this time, so try to measure your alcohol as well as what you say. Eat a few lighter foods than what you would usually.

27 Fri

Cast aside your financial concerns just now, because it is the festive season, after all. Revisit your banking problems when Christmas is over.

28 Sat

You desire a little freedom and want to break away from any constraints. This should be a great time for reuniting with friends, or you may travel.

29 Sun

You will reconnect with your spiritual belief system for a while around now. A rather unpleasant memory may trigger this.

30
Mon

As you near the end of the year, your fantasies and ambitions for increased professional satisfaction will be high on your agenda. Dream on.

31
Tues

Don't let work bother you just now, because it will be good to forget about it for the time being. Fortunately, a problem of a professional nature will work itself out without your intervention.

2012
ASTRONUMEROLOGY

EVERY MAN HAS IN HIMSELF A
CONTINENT OF UNDISCOVERED
CHARACTER. HAPPY IS HE WHO
ACTS AS THE COLUMBUS TO HIS
OWN SOUL.

Sir J. Stephen

THE POWER BEHIND ⊚ YOUR NAME ⊚

It's hard to believe that your name resonates with a numerical vibration, but it's true! Simply by adding together the numbers of your name, you can see which planet rules you and what effects your name will have on your life and destiny. According to the ancient Chaldean system of numerology, each number is assigned a planetary energy, and each alphabetical letter a number, as in the following list:

AIQJY	=	1	Sun
BKR	=	2	Moon
CGLS	=	3	Jupiter
DMT	=	4	Uranus
EHNX	=	5	Mercury
UVW	=	6	Venus
OZ	=	7	Neptune
FP	=	8	Saturn
—	=	9	Mars

Note: The number 9 is not allotted a letter because it was considered 'unknowable'.

Once the numbers have been added, you can establish which single planet rules your name and personal affairs. At this point the number 9 can be used for interpretation. Do you think it's unusual that many famous actors, writers and musicians modify their names? This is to attract luck and good fortune, which can be made easier by using the energies of a friendlier planet. Try experimenting with the table and see how new names affect you. It's so much fun, and you may even attract greater love, wealth and worldly success!

Look at the following example to work out the power of your name. A person named Andrew Brown would calculate his ruling planet by correlating each letter to a number in the table, like this:

A	N	D	R	E	W		B	R	O	W	N
1	5	4	2	5	6		2	2	7	6	5

And then add the numbers like this:

$1 + 5 + 4 + 2 + 5 + 6 + 2 + 2 + 7 + 6 + 5$	=	45
Then add	$4 + 5$ =	9

The ruling number of Andrew Brown's name is 9, which is governed by Mars (see how the 9 can now be used?). Now study the Name-Number Table to reveal the power of your name. The numbers 4 and 5 will play a secondary role in Andrew's character and destiny, so in his case you would also study the effects of Uranus (4) and Mercury (5).

Name Number	Ruling Planet	Name Characteristics
1	Sun	Attractive personality. Magnetic charm. Superman- or superwoman-like vitality and physical energy. Incredibly active and gregarious. Enjoys outdoor activities and sports. Has friends in powerful positions. Good government connections. Intelligent, spectacular, flashy and successful. A loyal number for love and relationships.
2	Moon	Feminine and soft, with an emotional temperament. Fluctuating moods but intuitive, possibly even has clairvoyant abilities. Ingenious nature. Expresses feelings kind-heartedly. Loves family, motherhood and home life. Night owl who probably needs more sleep. Success with the public and/or women generally.

Name Number	Ruling Planet	Name Characteristics
3	Jupiter	A sociable, optimistic number with a fortunate destiny. Attracts opportunities without too much effort. Great sense of timing. Religious or spiritual inclinations. Naturally drawn to investigating the meaning of life. Philosophical insight. Enjoys travel, explores the world and different cultures.
4	Uranus	Volatile character with many peculiar aspects. Likes to experiment and test novel experiences. Forward-thinking, with many extraordinary friends. Gets bored easily so needs plenty of inspiring activities. Pioneering, technological and creative. Wilful and obstinate at times. Unforeseen events in life may be positive or negative.

Name Number	Ruling Planet	Name Characteristics
5	Mercury	Sharp-witted and quick-thinking, with great powers of speech. Extremely active in life: always on the go and living on nervous energy. Has a youthful outlook and never grows old— looks younger than actual age. Has young friends and a humorous disposition. Loves reading and writing. Great communicator.
6	Venus	Delightful and charming personality. Graceful and eye-catching. Cherishes and nourishes friends. Very active social life. Musical or creative interests. Has great money-making opportunities as well as numerous love affairs. A career in the public eye is quite likely. Loves family, but often troubled over divided loyalties with friends.

Name Number	Ruling Planet	Name Characteristics
7	Neptune	Intuitive, spiritual and self-sacrificing nature. Easily duped by those who need help. Loves to dream of life's possibilities. Has healing powers. Dreams are revealing and prophetic. Loves the water and will have many journeys in life. Spiritual aspirations dominate worldly desires.
8	Saturn	Hard-working, ambitious person with slow yet certain achievements. Remarkable concentration and self-sacrifice for a chosen objective. Financially focused, but generous when a person's trust is gained. Proficient in his or her chosen field but a hard taskmaster. Demands perfection and needs to relax and enjoy life more.

Name Number	Ruling Planet	Name Characteristics
9	**Mars**	Extraordinary physical drive, desires and ambition. Sports and outdoor activities are major keys to health. Confrontational, but likes to work and play really hard. Protects and defends family, friends and territory. Has individual tastes in life, but is also self-absorbed. Needs to listen to others' advice to gain greater success.

YOUR PLANETARY
RULER

Astrology and numerology are intimately connected. Each planet rules over a number between 1 and 9. Both your name and your birth date are governed by planetary energies. As described earlier, here are the planets and their ruling numbers:

1   Sun

2   Moon

3   Jupiter

4   Uranus

5   Mercury

6   Venus

7   Neptune

8   Saturn

9   Mars

To find out which planet will control the coming year for you, simply add the numbers of your birth date and the year in question. An example follows.

If you were born on 14 November, add the numerals 1 and 4 (14, your day of birth) and 1 and 1 (11, your month of birth) to the year in question, in this case 2012 (current year), like this:

Add 1 + 4 + 1 + 1 + 2 + 0 + 1 + 2 = 12

1 + 2 = 3

Thus, the planet ruling your individual karma for 2012 would be Jupiter, because this planet rules the number 3.

YOUR PLANETARY
❂ FORECAST ❂

You can even take your ruling name number, as discussed previously, and add it to the year in question to throw more light on your coming personal affairs, like this:

A N D R E W B R O W N	=	9
Year coming	=	2012
Add 9 + 2 + 0 + 1 + 2	=	14
Add 1 + 4	=	5

Thus, this would be the ruling year number based on your name number. Therefore, you would study the influence of Mercury (5) using the Trends for Your Planetary Number table in 2012. Enjoy!

Trends for Your Planetary Number in 2012

Year Number	Ruling Planet	Results Throughout the Coming Year
1	Sun	**Overview**

Overview

The commencement of a new cycle: a year full of accomplishments, increased reputation and brand new plans and projects.

Many new responsibilities. Success and strong physical vitality. Health should improve and illnesses will be healed.

If you have ailments, now is the time to improve your physical wellbeing—recovery will be certain.

Love and pleasure

A lucky year for love. Creditable connections with children, family life is in focus. Music, art and creative expression will be fulfilling. New romantic opportunities.

Work

Minimal effort for maximum luck. Extra money and exciting opportunities professionally. Positive new changes result in promotion and pay rises.

Improving your luck

Luck is plentiful throughout the year, but especially in July and August. The 1st, 8th, 15th and 22nd hours of Sundays are lucky.

Lucky numbers are 1, 10, 19 and 28.

Year Number	Ruling Planet	Results Throughout the Coming Year
2	Moon	**Overview**

Overview

Reconnection with your emotions and past. Excellent for relationships with family members. Moodiness may become a problem. Sleeping patterns will be affected.

Love and pleasure

Home, family life and relationships are focused in 2012. Relationships improve through self-effort and greater communication. Residential changes, renovations and interior decoration bring satisfaction. Increased psychic sensitivity.

Work

Emotional in work. Home career, or hobby from a domestic base, will bring greater income opportunities. Females will be more prominent in your work.

Improving your luck

July will fulfil some of your dreams. Mondays will be lucky: the 1st, 8th, 15th and 22nd hours of them are the most fortunate. Pay special attention to the new and full Moons in 2012.

Lucky numbers include 2, 11, 20, 29 and 38.

Year Number	Ruling Planet	Results Throughout the Coming Year
3	Jupiter	

Overview

A lucky year for you. Exciting opportunities arise to expand horizons. Good fortune financially. Travels and increased popularity. A happy year. Spiritual, humanitarian and self-sacrificial focus. Self-improvement is likely.

Love and pleasure

Speculative in love. May meet someone new to travel with, or travel with your friends and lovers. Gambling results in some wins and some losses. Current relationships will deepen in their closeness.

Work

Fortunate for new opportunities and success. Employers are more accommodating and open to your creative expression. Extra money. Promotions are quite possible.

Improving your luck

Remain realistic, get more sleep and don't expect too much from your efforts. Planning is necessary for better luck. The 1st, 8th, 15th and 24th hours of Thursdays are spiritually very lucky for you.

Lucky numbers this year are 3, 12, 21 and 30. March and December are lucky months. The year 2012 will bring some unexpected surprises.

Year Number	Ruling Planet	Results Throughout the Coming Year
4	Uranus	

Overview

Unexpected events, both pleasant and sometimes unpleasant, are likely. Difficult choices appear. Break free of your past and self-imposed limitations. An independent year in which a new path will be forged. Discipline is necessary. Structure your life appropriately, even if doing so is difficult.

Love and pleasure

Guard against dissatisfaction in relationships. Need freedom and experimentation. May meet someone out of the ordinary. Emotional and sexual explorations. Spirituality and community service enhanced. Many new friendships.

Work

Progress is made in work. Technology and other computer or Internet-related industries are fulfilling. Increased knowledge and work skills. New opportunities arise when they are least expected. Excessive work and tension. Learn to relax. Efficiency in time essential. Work with groups and utilise networks to enhance professional prospects.

Year Number	Ruling Planet	Results Throughout the Coming Year
		Improving your luck
		Moderation is the key word. Be patient and do not rush things. Slow your pace this year, as being impulsive will only lead to errors and missed opportunities. Exercise greater patience in all matters. Steady investments are lucky.
		The 1st, 8th, 15th and 20th hours of any Saturday will be very lucky in 2012.
		Your lucky numbers are 4, 13, 22 and 31.

Year Number	Ruling Planet	Results Throughout the Coming Year
5	Mercury	**Overview**

Intellectual activities and communication increases. Imagination is powerful. Novel and exciting new concepts will bring success and personal satisfaction.

Goal-setting will be difficult. Acquire the correct information before making decisions. Develop concentration and stay away from distracting or negative people.

Love and pleasure

Give as much as you take in relationships. Changes in routine are necessary to keep your love life upbeat and progressive. Develop open-mindedness.

Avoid being critical of your partner. Keep your opinions to yourself. Artistic pursuits and self-improvement are factors in your relationships.

Work

Become a leader in your field in 2012. Contracts, new job offers and other agreements open up new pathways to success. Develop business skills.

Speed, efficiency and capability are your key words this year. Don't be impulsive in making any career changes. Travel is also on the agenda.

Year Number	Ruling Planet	Results Throughout the Coming Year

Improving your luck

Write ideas down, research topics more thoroughly, communicate enthusiasm through meetings—this will afford you much more luck. Stick to one idea.

The 1st, 8th, 15th and 20th hours of Wednesdays are luckiest, so schedule meetings and other important social engagements at these times.

Throughout 2012 your lucky numbers are 5, 14, 23 and 32.

Year Number	Ruling Planet	Results Throughout the Coming Year
6	Venus	**Overview**

Overview

A year of love. Expect romantic and sensual interludes, and new love affairs. Number 6 is also related to family life. Working with a loved one or family member is possible, with good results. Save money, cut costs. Share success.

Love and pleasure

The key word for 2012 is romance. Current relationships are deepened. New relationships will be formed and may have some karmic significance, especially if single. Spend time grooming and beautifying yourself: put your best foot forward. Engagement and even marriage is possible. Increased social responsibilities. Moderate excessive tendencies.

Work

Further interest in financial matters and future material security. Reduce costs and become frugal. Extra cash is likely. Additional income or bonuses are possible. Working from home may also be of interest. Social activities and work coincide.

Year Number	Ruling Planet	Results Throughout the Coming Year
		Improving your luck

Work and success depend on a creative and positive mental attitude. Eliminate bad habits and personal tendencies that are obstructive. Balance spiritual and financial needs.

The 1st, 8th, 15th and 20th hours on Fridays are extremely lucky this year, and new opportunities can arise when they are least expected.

The numbers 6, 15, 24 and 33 will generally increase your luck.

Year Number	Ruling Planet	Results Throughout the Coming Year
7	Neptune	**Overview**

Overview

An intuitive and spiritual year. Your life path becomes clear. Focus on your inner powers to gain a greater understanding and perspective of your true mission in life. Remove emotional baggage. Make peace with past lovers who have hurt or betrayed you. Forgiveness is the key word this year.

Love and pleasure

Spend time loving yourself, not just bending over backwards for others. Sacrifice to those who are worthy. Relationships should be reciprocal. Avoid deception, swindling or other forms of gossip. Affirm what you want in a relationship to your lover. Set high standards.

Work

Unselfish work is the key to success. Learn to say no to demanding employers or co-workers. Remove clutter to make space for bigger and better things. Healing and caring professions may feature strongly. Use your intuition to manoeuvre carefully into new professional directions.

Year Number	Ruling Planet	Results Throughout the Coming Year
		Improving your luck

Maintain cohesive lines of communication and stick to one path for best results. Pay attention to health and don't let stress affect a positive outlook. Sleep well, exercise and develop better eating habits to improve energy circulation.

The 1st, 8th, 15th and 20th hours of Wednesdays are luckiest, so schedule meetings and other important social engagements at these times.

Throughout 2012 your lucky numbers are 7, 16, 25 and 34.

Year Number	Ruling Planet	Results Throughout the Coming Year
8	Saturn	**Overview**

Overview

This is a practical year requiring effort, hard work and a certain amount of solitude for best results. Pay attention to structure, timelines and your diary. Don't try to help too many people, but rather, focus on yourself. This will be a year of discipline and self-analysis. However, income levels will eventually increase.

Love and pleasure

Balance personal affairs with work. Show affection to loved ones through practicality and responsibility.

Dedicate time to family, not just work. Schedule activities outdoors for increased wellbeing and emotional satisfaction.

Work

Money is on the increase this year, but continued focus is necessary. Hard work equals extra income. A cautious and resourceful year, but be generous where possible. Some new responsibilities will bring success. Balance income potential with creative satisfaction.

Year Number	Ruling Planet	Results Throughout the Coming Year
		Improving your luck

Being overcautious and reluctant to attempt something new will cause delay and frustration if new opportunities are offered. Be kind to yourself and don't overwork or overdo exercise. Send out positive thought-waves to friends and loved ones. The karmic energy will return.

The 1st, 8th, 15th and 20th hours of Saturdays are the best times for you in 2012.

The numbers 1, 8, 17, 26 and 35 are lucky.

Year Number	Ruling Planet	Results Throughout the Coming Year
9	Mars	

Overview

The ending of one chapter of your life and the preparation for the beginning of a new cycle. A transition period when things may be in turmoil or a state of uncertainty. Remain calm. Do not be impulsive or irritable. Avoid arguments. Calm communication will help find solutions.

Love and pleasure

Tremendous energy and drive help you achieve goals this year. But don't be too pushy when forcing your ideas down other people's throats, so to speak. Diplomatic discussions, rather than arguments, should be used to achieve outcomes. Discuss changes before making decisions with partners and lovers in your life.

Work

A successful year with the expectation of bigger and better things next year. Driven by work objectives or ambition. Tendency to overdo and overwork. Pace your deadlines. Leadership role likely. Respect and honour from your peers and employers.

Year Number	Ruling Planet	Results Throughout the Coming Year
		Improving your luck

Find adequate outlets for your high level of energy through meditation, self-reflection and prayer. Collect your energies and focus them on one point. Release tension to maintain health.

The 1st, 8th, 15th and 20th hours of Tuesdays will be lucky for you throughout 2012.

Your lucky numbers are 9, 18, 27 and 36.